# Learn Coding with Python

*How to Use Python Programming Language Hands-On Machine Learning Projects for Complete Beginners (Data Science from Scratch)*

# Table of Contents

# Introduction

Congratulations on purchasing *Learn Coding with Python* and thank you for doing so.

The following chapters will discuss all of the different parts that you need to know when it comes to coding in the Python language, and how to handle some of the tasks that machine learning will throw your way. There are many benefits to working with Python, whether you are a programmer or just someone learning to pick up a new skill, and it is one of the best coding languages out there for handling any machine learning process that you want. And this guidebook is going to show you the exact steps you can take to use Python machine learning for all of your needs.

To start this guidebook, we are going to spend some time exploring machine learning and what is all about. We will take a look at some of the benefits of machine learning, how machine learning works, the importance of machine learning for many businesses across a variety of industries, and even some of the most common types of machine learning. These will include examples of supervised, unsupervised, and reinforcement machine learning.

With this in mind, we are going to move on to an introduction of Python and how it can be used along with machine learning to get our projects done. We will look at the benefits of Python and how it can work with machine learning in particular, and then expand out to some of the best libraries to work with when you want to handle a data science or machine learning project.

From here, we will spend time learning about the process of data analysis. There are actually quite a few steps that have to happen to gain insights out of any data that is collected, and it isn't just about collecting the data. We will take a look at some of the other important steps, including cleaning the data, analyzing the data, and more. When this is done, anyone will be able to step up and use the data they have collected to help them make smarter business decisions.

This guidebook will end with some of the best Python machine learning algorithms that you can use to help your system or machine sort through data and give you the insights and predictions that you are looking for. We will take a look at how to find the support vector machine, working with neural networks, K-Nearest Neighbors, and even some clustering examples.

Machine learning has become a buzz word in almost all industries of business, and many of those who run these companies are looking to see how they can benefit from the ideas and technologies that come with it. And Python is the best programming language to use to make all of these projects happen with machine learning. When you are ready to use machine learning for the benefit of your company, and you want to use Python to make it happen, check out this guidebook to get started.

There are plenty of books on this subject on the market, thanks again for choosing this one! Every effort was made to ensure it is full of as much useful information as possible, please enjoy it!

# Chapter 1: An Introduction to Machine Learning

The first topic that we need to take some time to explore is going to be machine learning. Machine learning is a subset of artificial intelligence, so we are going to see a lot of overlapping and similarities between the two topics as we go along. Machine learning is a process that has been around for some time, but with the growth of data science and the collection of Big Data by many companies, it is becoming a big name for many industries.

To keep it simple, machine learning is going to be one of the main methods of data analysis that is responsible for automating the building of analytical models. It is going to be one of the branches that come with artificial intelligence, and it is based on the idea that a machine or a system is able to learn from data, make decisions on its own without much intervention from humans, and even identify some of the patterns that are found in the data.

With machine learning, you are teaching the computer or the program to use its own experiences with the user in the past in order to perform better in the future. An example of this would be a program that can help with spam email filtering. There are a few methods that can work in this instance, but the easiest one would be to teach the computer how to categorize, memorize, and then identify all the emails in your inbox that you label as spam when they enter your email. Then, if some new emails come in later that match what is already on your email list, the program would be able to mark these as spam without any work on your part.

While this kind of memorization method is the easiest technique to program and work with, there are still some things that will be lacking with it. First of all, you are missing out on the inductive reasoning in the program, which needs to be there for efficient learning. As a programmer, it is much better to go through and program the computer so that it can learn how to discern the message types that come in and that are spam, rather than trying to get the program to memorize the information.

There are so many different things that we are able to do when it comes to machine learning, and taking the time to really explore them and understand what is there can be important as well. So, let's dive right in and explore more about what we can do with the help of machine learning and some of the algorithms that come with it as well.

## The History of Machine Learning

Thanks to some of the brand-new technologies in computing that are becoming more mainstream, machine learning has been able to benefit and change a lot of businesses and the way that they create products and reach their customers. Machine learning traditionally was born just from the idea of pattern recognition and the theory that we could get systems, machines, and computers, to learn without being programmed to perform a specific task.

The start of machine learning comes from researchers who were interested in artificial intelligence. These individuals wanted to take the ideas that came with artificial intelligence and then see if it were possible to train a computer to learn from the data present, without the programmer having to go through and code out all of the different parts along the way. With artificial intelligence and the help of various models and algorithms with machine learning, the systems that we use today can learn on their own.

The iterative aspect that is a big part of machine learning can be important because as a model is exposed to some new data, these models will be able to adapt on their own, without a lot of coding and programmer from a person. These models are able to learn from some of the previous computations to produce results and decisions that we are able to rely on, and that we could repeat later if needed. Machine learning is not really new science, and some of the ideas that come with it have been around for some time. This is, however, a science that has gained a lot of fresh momentum in the process.

While there are quite a few algorithms that fit under the term of machine learning, and some of these have been around for a long time, the ability to automatically apply complex mathematical calculations to big data, over and over, faster, and faster, is a more recent development. And because of this, there are many companies who are jumping on board, trying to see how they can use it for their own needs.

## The Benefits of Machine Learning

There are a number of benefits that we are able to see when it comes to working with machine learning and all of the neat tools and techniques that come with it. Many businesses are jumping on board with what this process can do, and no matter what your goals are, or what industry you work with, machine learning is going to be able to help you out. Some of the benefits that companies are able to experience when it comes to machine learning will include:

First, companies are able to work with machine learning in order to increase their customer satisfaction. When the company is able to learn more about its customers, and what the customer is looking for, it is easier to meet these needs and see a higher level of customer satisfaction. The machine learning algorithms that we talk about later, with the help of a lot of big data, can provide us with insights about the customer and what the customer would like.

It can help them to beat out the competition. Competition is fierce in almost any industry that is out there. something as simple as gathering data and then doing an analysis can help you to figure out new ways to corner the market, new niches to get into, and so much more. You have to make sure that you are sorting through the right data, and that you choose the right algorithm, but overall this is going to be a great way to figure out how to remain on top, or at least get a bigger piece of the pie.

Is a great way to figure out which products to market next When you can learn more about what the customer and the market, it is easier to know which products are likely to take off, and which ones are a waste of time. By collecting data about many different parts of the product, and comparing it to the wants of the customers, and maybe other products that are on the market, or that have been released in the past, the machine learning algorithm can help the business make a prediction on how well that product will do.

It can help create a better marketing campaign. Marketing is so important to many companies because it ensures that their customers will be able to find them and that they can see an increase in sales. With the right predictions and insights from a machine learning model, the company can learn more about their customers, about the market, and about their target demographics and can make better and smarter decisions about how to complete a marketing campaign.

It helps the business to cut down on waste and increase profits. Many companies are interested in using machine learning as a way to reduce waste in their company, whether it is waste in materials, waste in time for doing a process, or even waste because a piece of equipment fails and it cuts into production time to fix it. All of these are things that machine learning can help to fix. For example, several manufacturing companies have used machine learning to figure out when a machine part is likely to need replacing. They can then schedule that replacement, before the part breaks, and at a time that is more convenient to not ruin production time.

Machine learning can also be used in some of the products that a company creates. Things like search engines, Google's self-driving car, and various voice recognition devices like our cell phones, Amazon Echo, and more, are examples of how this can happen. A company can use some of the technology that comes with machine learning in order to create their own devices and products, and then market that technology as well.

## Why Do We Need to Use Machine Learning?

It is likely that at one point or another, you have heard about machine learning. Anyone who is running a business and gathering up data to use for later will hear about machine learning and all of the neat things that it is able to do for your business. In reality, while it is nice that you have been able to spend some time searching for data and seeing what you are able to collect overall, this is not enough. That data is worthless to you, and a big waste of money if you are not able to sort through it and see what it says, and what insights are present inside of it.

This is where machine learning is going to come into play. You can spend all day working with the data, collecting it, and hoping that it will provide you with some good insights, but if you don't actually take a look at the information and see what is there, then you are going to be in trouble. Gathering and storing the data isn't going to do you much good. Gathering and analyzing the data will. And machine learning is able to help you get all of this done.

This is why machine learning has become such a prevalent idea in the business world, no matter what industry you are currently in. machine learning is able to help you to produce models quickly and automatically, models that are able to analyze bigger and more complex data while delivering results that are more accurate, and results that are done quickly, compared to the past. And all of this can be scalable, so no matter how large the data is that you want to work with, machine learning and some of the models that you create from it can be your friend.

When you use machine learning, you can build up precise models as we talked about above. By building up these precise models, a company is going to see a lot of benefits, and they are given the chance to identify profitable opportunities, or even avoid some of the risks that are unknown in the beginning.

Of course, there are a lot of different algorithms and models that you are able to create when it comes to working with machine learning. And being able to handle all of these, and knowing which ones are right for the job, will definitely depend on the data that you want to analyze which one will be the best for your data analysis.

There are a number of applications that we are able to work with when it comes to how we can use machine learning. As we start working with some of the parts with machine learning, you may notice that there is a lot of change that comes with the topic over the years, and there are a ton of unique and fun things that a programmer is able to do with this kind of learning to see the most benefits.

As this topic starts to grow, and we are able to see more and more what this kind of technology and the models that we are working within machine learning, we will find that more companies will work with machine learning will increase at a steady rate, and there will be more applications of machine learning as the time goes on. While there are quite a few applications out there already that machine learning is able to help these companies see success, but some of the most common methods that happen with machine learning will include some of the following:

- **Statistical research:** machine learning is a big part of IT now. You will find that machine learning will help you to go through a lot of complexity when looking through large data patterns. Some of the options that will use statistical research include search engines, credit cards, and filtering spam messages.

- **Big data analysis:** many companies need to be able to get through a lot of data in a short amount of time. They use this data to recognize how their customers spend money and even to make decisions and predictions about the future. This used to take a long time to have someone sit through and look at the data, but now machine learning can do the process faster and much more efficiently. Options like election campaigns, medical fields, and retail stores have used machine learning for this purpose.
- **Finances:** some finance companies have also used machine learning. Stock trading online has seen a rise in the use of machine learning to help make efficient and safe decisions and so much more.

As we talked about a bit before, these are just going to include a few of the ways that we are able to work with machine learning in order to grow a business. This is a technology that is taking over the world, and it will not be long before we see that it can start to creep into so many more parts of our world that we need to focus on as well.

# What Industries Are Benefitting from Machine Learning?

While machine learning may sound like a crazy process that isn't going to work, and that, while it is a nice theory, it is not something that we are able to benefit from, there are actually quite a few businesses out there already we are working with data science and some of the great processes that it can help with. Most of the industries out there that work with large amounts of data have already been able to recognize how valuable the technology of machine learning can be for them. By gleaning insights out of this data, and this can often be done in real-time, organizations are able to work more efficiently than before, and gain a nice advantage over their competition.

Almost any and every industry out there is able to benefit in some way from machine learning. Whether this machine learning is used to help grow the business, to help them understand their customers better, or even to help create a brand-new product, machine learning can be there to help. Some of the companies and industries who are relying on machine learning right now to help their business include:

The world of finances. There are a lot of different transactions and applications and more than a bank and other financial institutions need to keep track of on a regular basis. This is part of how they conduct their business, and their customers, especially those who have an account with them, want to make sure that their money is always safe and sound. But there are just so many transactions that are going on at the same time, from bank withdrawals to deposits, from loan applications to credit card purchases, that it is sometimes hard for these businesses to keep up with everything.

This is where machine learning can come into play. There are already a number of models in place in the financial world that rely on machine learning, and it is likely that this trend is going to keep on growing. Fraud detection is one example. This model is able to collect information on other fraud attempts that happened in the accounts in the past and can use that information to detect when something seems off with the account of a user. These are also used to help banks offer the best products and services to their customers, and to help choose who is eligible for a loan or not.

The government can also benefit from using machine learning in many cases. Many of the agencies that fall under the government, including utilities and public safety, can really benefit from using the models that come with machine learning as their own. For example, these agencies can work with the data they receive from sensor data to figure out how to increase efficiency and save money in the process.

Next on the list is the world of health care. There may not be a field that is able to benefit more from machine learning and all it has to offer than the health care field. From helping doctors to make a diagnosis on their patients faster, to using sensors to monitor a patient a little bit better when the nurses are short on staff and can't make it everywhere, to even using virtual assistants to help deal with patients, machine learning is already taking the health care industry by storm and is likely to grow.

This is one place where a lot of people are worried that machine learning is going to swoop in and take all the jobs. But this is not the point of machine learning. Remember that we are working with machines and algorithms and that these, no matter how much they can help us, are not meant to replace people in their jobs. But where there are industries that can't get through all of that information in an efficient manner, or where there are going to be too many job openings and not enough applications, the machine learning algorithms that run the various techniques could be helpful.

Oil and gas is another industry that is able to work with the models of machine learning to see some results. There are a number of ways that machine learning is able to help out with the world of oil and gas. Machine learning can help these companies to find new sources of energy, to analyze some of the minerals in the ground, to predict when one of the sensors in the refinery is going to fail, and finding ways to make the process of distributing oil more streamlined than before. There are already a lot of uses for machine learning in this field, and it is likely that they will expand more in the future.

The retail industry is able to benefit quite a bit when it comes to all that machine learning is able to do. These companies may not focus on engineering, mathematics, or science like a few of the others do, but these retail businesses are still collecting a ton of data on their customers, and when they use that data in the right manner, it is going to help them to increase their sales and customer satisfaction in the process.

One example of how the retail industry is able to benefit from machine learning is with a website that recommends items to a customer, or a potential customer, based on what they purchased in the past. Machine learning is used in order to analyze the buying history of that customer before making the recommendations that are needed.

Retailers are going to rely on all of the different parts of machine learning in order to capture the data they need, analyze that data, and then use the data to make some personalized shopping recommendations. This data can also be used to implement a good marketing campaign, to optimize the prices for the customer and the business, to help provide insights on the customer, and to help with merchandise supply planning.

And finally, we can look at how the industry of transportation can work with machine learning as well. Being able to analyze a large amount of data and then identify some of the patterns and trends that are there can be key to the transportation industry. This is an industry that is reliant on making routes more efficient, and being able to predict ahead of time potential problems can help to increase how much profit is made.

The modeling aspect, along with the process of data analysis, is going to be an important tool used for public transportation, delivery companies, and some of the other organizations that focus on transportation as well. And all of these tools are examples of what machine learning is able to do for us.

## Machine Learning, Data Mining, and Deep Learning

When you are first trying to learn a bit more about data analysis and machine learning, it may seem like there are a lot of terms that seem very similar, and it is hard to know what the similarities and differences between them are. For example, data mining, deep learning, and machine learning all seem to have a similar definition as each other.

Although these three methods are going to be presented to us with the same goal, which is to extract the patterns, relationships, and insights out of a big source of data to make some decisions, they are going to come with different abilities of what they can do, and different approaches to how they are going to get this all done. Let's take a closer look at each one to see how these are different at getting a similar goal completed.

First on the list is data mining. This is going to be more of a superset of many methods that a data scientist can use to take data and extract all of the insights out of it. When someone attempts to work with data mining, it is going to involve the process of traditional statistical methods and machine learning. Data mining is able to apply methods from many different areas to identify previously unknown patterns that are hiding in your data. This can include a lot of things like text analytics, machine learning, time series analysis, and statistical algorithms. Data mining, in addition to all that we have above, is going to include the study and the practice of data manipulation and storage for our needs.

In contrast to this, we have machine learning. The main difference here is that just like with the statistical models, the goal is for us to understand the structure of the data, fit theoretical distributions to the data that we already understand. So, with the models that are statistical, there is a theory behind any model we have been able to prove mathematically, but before this theory can be shown, there is the requirement that the data can meet up with some strong assumptions as well.

Machine learning has developed based on the ability to use a computer to look through and probe the data that we have for a good structure, even if we are going through that data without a food theory of what our structure actually looks like. The test that we use for this kind of model with machine learning is a validation error on the new data, rather than a theoretical test that proves a hypothesis that is null. Because machine learning is able to use an approach that is more iterative to learn from the data, the learning can be automated pretty easily. Passes are run through this data as many times as it takes until a robust pattern can be found.

Then we have deep learning. This process is going to combine together the advances that are necessary in computing power and special types of neural networks in order to help learn complicated patterns in large amounts of data that it has. The techniques that go with this one are considered the state of the art when it comes to identifying objects that are found in images, and words out of sounds.

Right now, there is research being done that looks to apply these successes in pattern recognition to more complex tasks, including medical diagnoses, automatic language translation, and other important business and social problems that need some assistance.

# How Machine Learning Works

The last thing that we need to take a look at in this guidebook is how machine learning is going to work. To make sure that you can use this process and get the most out of it, you have to know how to pair the best algorithms with the right tools and process along the way. There are many tools and processes that we are able to pull out and use in machine learning, but often it seems overwhelming and like we will never be able to figure out how it all works

While machine learning is a more complex form of programming, it is not designed to be hard or difficult to learn. Instead, when we can combine some of the Python programming language (which we will talk about a bit more later), with the algorithms and models of machine learning, we will see all of this come into place.

The main part of machine learning that ensures that it gets up and running well is the algorithms. There are different algorithms that come into play, ensuring that machine learning performs the task that you would like. But these are the basics that help us to sort through all of that data and come up with the predictions and the insights that we need overall. It is as simple to work with like that!

The right graphical user interface that can be used with machine learning is going to be really helpful here. You will be able to use that interface to build up some models for machine learning and even implement some of the iterative processes of machine learning that you would like. You don't have to be an advanced statistician to do this. With the right algorithms, and some good data science and machine learning libraries that we will talk about later, anyone can input the data they need and get the machine learning algorithm to work.

While we will talk about a few of these algorithms later on as we go through this guidebook, there are a few that are pretty common, and it is worth your time to learn how they work and what they are. Some of the most common machine learning algorithms that beginners and more advanced programmers are going to work with include neural networks, decision trees, random forests, support vector machines, self-organizing maps, k-means clustering, nearest-neighbor mapping and more.

There are also a lot of different processes and tools that work with those algorithms to make sure we see the results that we are expecting. The algorithms can handle a lot of what we are doing here, but the biggest secret to getting the most value from that Big data you have been collecting is when you pair the algorithms with the right tools and processes for the task that you are trying to accomplish. Some of the best tools and processes that you can rely on here will include:

1. Comprehensive data management and quality.
2. GUIs to make sure that we can build up our models and handle the process flows.
3. Interactive data exploration and visualization of the results of the models that we create.
4. Comparisons of different models of machine learning to help us figure out which model is the best, as quickly as possible.
5. Automated ensemble model evaluation that will help us to identify the best performers overall.
6. Easy model deployment so that we can get results that can be repeated, and are reliable, in a quick and efficient manner.
7. An integrated, end to end platform for the automation of the data to the decision process.

As you can see, there are a lot of different parts that have to come together in order to ensure that machine learning behaves the way that we want. There is so much that machine learning is able to help us to do, and it is so important to use these algorithms and models to really get a good understanding of all the data we hold onto.

Many businesses are already gathering and holding onto a lot of data. And as more data becomes available, and various storage options for holding onto that data expand and are offered for a lower price, it is likely that this is a trend that will continue. You can gather all of the information and data that you want though, and still not see success if you don't take the time to really analyze that data and learn what insights and predictions are hidden inside.

This is where machine learning is going to come into play. It is designed to help us actually do the analysis of our data, and see what information may be hidden way down in it. This machine learning, with the right algorithms in place, can help us to make models that are trained on the information, and then tested, and from there it can make predictions, and give us sound business decision-making help that can propel us forward.

Every industry, no matter what they do to help the customer, can benefit when it comes to utilizing machine learning for their needs. And learning what machine learning is all about, and some of the neat things that you are able to do with it can make analyzing and understanding the Big Data you already have, easier than ever before.

# Chapter 2: The Different Types of Machine Learning

When we take a look at machine learning and all of the neat things that a business can do with it, it is no wonder that so many people have fallen in love with adding this to their business. Whether you want to use some of the algorithms from machine learning to help create a new product to put on the market, or you want to use machine learning to sort through all the data you have and learn how to make better decisions, machine learning can step right in and make all of this happen.

With that in mind, there are a few different types of machine learning that we are able to focus on. Each of these comes with their own algorithms and will teach the system or the machine that you are working in a different way. Each of these categories can be strong and will provide us with the learning that is needed, based on the kind of project that you would like to create.

There are four main types of learning that we can focus on machine learning. As you create your own model, you will better be able to tell which one of these algorithms is the best for you and your needs. These four types of learning are going to include supervised learning, unsupervised learning, semi-supervised learning, and reinforcement learning. Let's dive in and see what all of these are about, how they work, and when you would need to use each one for your needs.

## Supervised Machine Learning

The first type of machine learning algorithm that we are going to take a look at is known as supervised machine learning. There are a variety of algorithms that we are able to use when it comes to supervised machine learning, but with this one, we need to have lots of labeled and classified data to see the results.

With any algorithms that fit into the category of supervised machine learning, we can apply them in order to remember what the model learned in the past over to a new set of data, using some examples that have been labeled to predict events in the future.

This is a process that is similar to what we may see with teaching someone a new subject. You would show them examples of what works for that situation, and what doesn't. And then you will test them to see how much of the information they have been able to retain. From there, the person will be able to go through and pull up from what they learned in the past and use that for situations that meet them in the future.

This is similar to what we will see with machines and systems that rely on supervised machine learning. Starting from a good analysis of a known set of data for training, the learning algorithm is able to come up and produce an inferred function to help us make some good predictions about the values that will be the output.

The system that we are working with here is able to provide us with some targets to handle any of the new input, as long as you were able to do a sufficient amount of training ahead of time. In addition, the supervised machine learning algorithm is going to compare its output with the correct, and the intended output, to help find errors to make the right modifications to the model at the right times.

Supervised learning is going to occur when you pick out an algorithm that is able to learn the right response to the data a user input to it. There are several ways that supervised machine learning can do this. It can look at examples and other targeted responses that you provide to the computer. You could include values or strings of labels to help the program learn the right way to behave.

This is a simple process to work with, but an example to look at is when a teacher is teaching their students a new topic and they will show the class examples of the situation. The students would then learn how to memorize these examples because the examples will provide general rules about the topic. Then, when they see these examples, or things that are similar, they know how to respond. However, if an example is shown that isn't similar to what the class was shown, then they know how to respond as well.

When it comes to the learning algorithms that you can use with supervised machine learning, there are a few types that you can pick from. The most common types include:

- Decision trees
- Regression algorithms
- KNN
- Random forest

## Unsupervised Machine Learning

The second type of machine learning algorithm that we are able to work with is known as unsupervised machine learning. This one is going to work in a manner that is different than supervised machine learning, but some of the neat things that it is able to handle for us and some of the ways that it can handle data will really make a world of difference as well.

The algorithms that fit in with the category will be used when the information that we want to use to help train our models are not labeled or classified at all. The algorithms of unsupervised learning are going to study how a system or a machine is able to infer a function to describe some of the hidden structure from the data that is not labeled. This can save some time and money for the company but will ensure that the business can get the work done.

The system that is using unsupervised machine learning is not going to figure out the right output like with supervised learning. Instead, it is going to explore the data that is present and then will draw some inferences from the set of data to help describe any of those hidden structures that are found in any data presented to the model, especially the data that doesn't have a label on it.

There are a number of processes that we can work with when it comes to unsupervised learning. If you have ever worked with a search engine, then you have worked with an example of unsupervised machine learning. The program is able to learn based on the results the user chooses and will get better at bringing up more results that the user will like. It is impossible for a programmer to go through and estimate what each customer or user wants ahead of time, but the algorithm can do this for it.

Then there is the idea of voice recognition. Each person is going to use different words, and there are a variety of languages and dialects that are present in it. Trying to program the speech recognition device to be ready for everything would take forever and would not be efficient. But with unsupervised machine learning, the programmer would be able to get all of this done.

Unsupervised learning is the type that will happen when your algorithm is able to learn either from mistakes or examples without having an associated response that goes with it. What this means is that with these algorithms, they will be in charge of figuring out and analyzing the data patterns based on the input that you give it.

Now, there will also be a few different types of algorithms that can work well with unsupervised machine learning. Whichever algorithm you choose to go with, it is able to take that data and restructure it so that all the data will fall into classes. This makes it much easier for you to look over that information later. Unsupervised machine learning is often the one that you will use because it can set up the computer to do most of the work without requiring a human being there and writing out all the instructions for the computer.

A good example of this is if your company wants to read through a ton of data in order to make predictions about that information. It can also be used in most search engines to give accurate results.

There are a lot of different techniques that you can use when it comes to machine learning. Some of the most common methods include:

- Markov algorithm
- Clustering algorithm
- Neural networks

## Semi-Supervised Machine Learning

The third type of machine learning algorithm that we will focus on here is known as semi-supervised machine learning. This one is meant to combine the benefits of supervised machine learning and unsupervised machine learning, and can help to keep some of the costs down when you work with machine learning overall for your business.

Semi-supervised machine learning is going to fall somewhere between supervised and unsupervised machine learning since both of these are going to use labeled and also unlabeled data for training. In most cases, the amount of labeled data is going to be smaller than the amount of unlabeled data that you decide to use. This is due to the fact that labeled data is harder to gather and much more expensive, so it often doesn't make a lot of economic sense to gather as much of this.

However, companies recognize that labeled data can help them make better learning algorithms. The machine is able to learn faster when it sees labels on the data, we are presenting to it, so there is some value in using the labeled data over the unlabeled data. The unlabeled data though is often cheaper to work with, and easier to find, so for most businesses, finding a nice balance between the two can give them the results that they want, while keeping costs down.

The various machines and systems that rely on the semi-supervised machine learning algorithms are going to be able to improve their accuracy of learning considerably. Usually, semi-supervised learning is going to be chosen when we want to acquire labeled data, but doing so is going to require skilled and relevant resources to train and learn to form it, and maybe the business doesn't have these kinds of resources in the first place.

This kind of learning is going to bring in the best of both worlds many times. You can cut down on some of the skills and resources that are needed to work on the model, but still get the benefit of working with some of the supervised machine learning that we talked about before. For companies that have some trained data but can't afford the cost or the time to find more, or for those who would like to keep their costs to a minimum to start, semi-supervised machine learning is going to be the best option to choose.

# Reinforcement Machine Learning

The fourth type of machine learning that we need to focus on here is the reinforcement machine learning. This is a learning method that can interact with the environment around it by producing actions, and also discovering the errors and the rewards that are needed. A good way to think about this process is that the system learns based on a trial and error formula, much like humans do in our day to day life.

Trial and error, along with delayed reward, are going to be the more relevant characteristics that we can see with this kind of machine learning. This method is helpful because it is going to allow software agents and machines to automatically, without a lot of interference from a programmer or someone else, to determine the ideal behavior based on a specific context. The reason that the program wants to do this is to maximize its performance.

For this kind of machine learning algorithm to do its job properly, we need to make sure that the system or machine is set up with simple reward feedback. This allows the agent to learn which actions to take, and which ones are the best. This positive, or simple reward feedback, is going to be called the reinforcement signal. Without it, the program is not going to behave in the manner that you would like and it will struggle between knowing when to behave in a certain way or not.

There are some people who see reinforcement learning as the same thing as unsupervised learning because they are so similar, but it is important to understand that they are different. First, the input that is given to these algorithms will need to have some mechanisms for feedback. You can set these up to be either negative or positive based on the algorithm that you decide to write out.

So, whenever you decide to work with reinforcement machine learning, you are working with an option that is like trial and error. Think about when you are working with a younger child. When they do some action that you don't approve of, you will start by telling them to stop or you may put them in time out or do some other action to let them know that what they did is not fine. But, if that same child does something that you see as good, you will praise them and give them a ton of positive reinforcement. Through these steps, the child is learning what is acceptable behavior and what isn't.

To keep it simple, this is what reinforcement machine learning is going to be like. It works on the idea of trial and error and it requires that the application uses an algorithm that helps it to make decisions. It is a good one to go with any time that you are working with an algorithm that should make these decisions without any mistakes and with a good outcome. Of course, it is going to take some time for your program to learn what it should do. But you can add this to the specific code that you are writing so that your computer program leans how you want it to behave.

Machine learning is a great process because of all the neat things it can undertake, and how great it can be at helping a business be successful. While there is so much that this machine learning is able to do, it is best known for how it can enable an analysis of the massive amounts of data companies are taking in on a regular basis. While it generally is going to deliver faster and more accurate results to help a company find out where more of the risks are hidden and which opportunities are the most profitable, it does take some time and some additional resources in order to train in the proper manner.

When we combine machine learning with things like cognitive technologies and artificial intelligence, we are able to make the whole process more effective at handling and analyzing large volumes of information in the process. And adding in one of the four machine learning technologies that we have listed above can be the difference you are looking for as well.

Supervised, unsupervised, semi-supervised, and reinforcement machine learning are completely different types of learning processes that we can work with, but they still come up with the same goal of helping businesses analyze a large amount of data. Often the decision is going to come down to what you would like the machine or the system to do when everything is all said and done. This can lead you to which algorithm is the best for your needs, and which one you should focus your attention on the most.

Machine learning is becoming a big buzz word in the world of business, and this is for good reason. Businesses are already collecting a ton of information on their industry, on their competition, on their customers, and even on their own business operations. But this data is going to be worthless if they are not able to sort through all the information and see what is there. With the help of machine learning, it is easier to sort through that data and see what insights are present, and that does nothing but benefit a business!

# Chapter 3: The Python Coding Language and How It Works with Machine Learning

Now that we have had some time to look at what machine learning is all about, and how it can be used to benefit a business and help them handle their Big Data, it is time to move on to the coding language that is going to help make all of this happen!

Machine learning is going to be a process from artificial intelligence that takes all of the data a company has collected and then analyzes it. This ensures that the company is able to learn what valuable information is in that data, and they can then use it to make predictions about the future, and make smart business decisions in the process.

Then we can add in some Python coding. This is the part that makes machine learning works and helps to drive all of the different types of learning that we talked about in the previous chapter. It is the coding that we need to use in order to actually sort through the data that we have, and then will present us with the results in the end. We will look at some of the algorithms and the steps that we can take to make this happen with Python, but for now, let's take a look at how Python works and why it is one of the best coding languages to use with machine learning.

There are a lot of programmers out there who like the idea of working with Python compared to some of the other languages out there, and some of the features that come with the Python language will make it more effective at handling some of the more complex parts that come with machine learning overall.

The number one thing that beginners are going to like when it comes to coding in Python, especially those who have been hiding away from coding in any language because they think it is too difficult is that the Python is considered an object-oriented programming language, or OOP. This may not make much sense to someone who is not in the world of programming on a regular basis, but it is the key that you need to make programming much easier in the long run.

In the past, the coding could be difficult because some of the organization was not as good as it should be. Things would move around and not stay put in the places where they were supposed to. New programmers who were working on the coding language had a steep learning curve, and this just added to some of the frustration. When nothing would stay where it was supposed to and it was hard to call things back up, many would give up in frustration.

With the Python coding language, this is not something that holds the same issue any longer. The OOP language is able to take classes and use these to hold onto a lot of the objects that are created inside that code. And because the objects are based on real-life items that we can feel and touch, and the classes keep everything in place, this makes it easier to write code and know all of the parts will stay in one place.

So, for those who have been worried about working with a coding language at all, this is no longer a big concern to worry about. Python makes it easier to handle the coding, which can add in a bit of courage to make this easier to handle some of the more complex tasks that you want to do with machine learning. With this factor, as well as some of the other benefits that come with the Python language, and some of the great libraries that happen to go with Python, you will be able to handle all of the different parts that come with any machine learning algorithm or model.

With that in mind, it is time to take a closer look at the Python language, some of the benefits that come with this language, and the exact way that this language better than any of the other coding languages out there, can help us to complete some of our machine learning tasks.

## The Benefits of the Python Language

Python is a language that a lot of programmers, beginners and more advanced, are interested in learning about. This is because there are a lot of benefits that come with this language. Some of the benefits that many programmers enjoy about the Python language include:

It is easy to learn how to use. If you are just getting started with coding, and you want to jump right in with machine learning, then Python is the coding language for your needs. It is set up to make programming and coding easier for everyone and will ensure that even as a beginner, you are going to be able to get the results that you want with coding. Python is able to take some of the complex topics, even those of machine learning, and can make them easier to work with.

You will find that as we work through some of the codes below for creating our own machine learning algorithms with Python, that if you know some of the basics of Python, you will still be able to recognize some of the basic parts. This is part of the beauty that comes with Python machine learning and will ensure that beginners and more advanced coders will be able to handle any machine learning task that they want.

There are a number of libraries, and many works with machine learning and data science. The basic library that comes with Python has a lot of the power and strength that you need, and there are a ton of options that you will enjoy just by coding in this language. But there are still a few tasks and projects that you won't be able to do without some other extensions and libraries present to take on the work.

This is especially true when it comes to Python and machine learning. The good news here is that Python comes with a number of extensions and libraries that are specifically designed to work with machine learning and data science. You simply need to go through the necessary steps to install those on your computer, and then you can start using them right away for your machine learning models and projects.

It can work with other coding languages. There are times when you need to combine Python together with another language in order to get the end results that are necessary to accomplish many tasks, including some of the tasks that you want to do with machine learning. Several of the libraries that we will talk about in a bit, for example, will let you code in Python, but then execute the commands in another language.

The fact that Python is able to work with other languages, and can be executed in another language, is pretty amazing. This ensures that you can get that extra boost of power, or that needed compatibility, without having to change up your coding language or learn another language to get started. Python is able to handle this and can make coding for beginners and more advanced programmers so much easier.

It has enough power to handle some of the machine learning projects and models that you need. Even though we just spent some time talking about how the Python language has been designed with the beginner in mind, you don't have to worry that it won't have enough strength behind it to handle some of the projects that you want. Python has plenty of power, and when you add in some of the extensions and libraries that are present with this language, you will find that it has plenty of power to handle even the most complex machine learning models that you want to create.

It has a nice community to work with if you get stuck or need help troubleshooting. Because there are so many people who like to work with the Python language, it makes sense that there would be a large community. As a beginner, you can use this community to learn new libraries and coding, get answers to some of the questions that you have as you work along, and advice on what to do when you run into some trouble with your program.

Since machine learning is a more complex application of the Python language, it is a great thing that we can come to rely on this community to help us get through all of it. You can get advice on how to handle the machine learning problem that you are working on right now and learn some new things at the same time as well.

There are a lot of benefits that come with Python when you want to use it to help out with some of the work that you are doing in machine learning. Some coders and programmers like to bring in another language to help them get things done. But none of those other languages are going to bring in the ease of use and the strength to handle machine learning as we will see with the Python coding language.

## How Does Python Work with Machine Learning?

There are a lot of benefits that come with using Python as a whole, no matter what kind of programming you want to work on. It has a ton of libraries to work with, is easy enough for a beginner to learn, and enough power to handle almost any task that you need, including machine learning. While there may be many other programming and coding languages that you can work with to complete machine learning, none of them are as widely used and beneficial as Python.

The Python programming language is going to be a great option to work with when it comes to machine learning. There are a number of reasons why Python is a popular choice with any professional who works on a system that relies on machine learning, no matter what industry they are in. one of the most commonly cited reasons for this use is the syntax of Python. This syntax is described in many ways, but the two features that help it work with machine learning is that the syntax is both math-like and elegant.

Expert in the field points out that some of the semantics of Python have a correspondence to some mathematical ideas that are common, so it isn't going to take a huge learning curve to apply some of this mathematics over to the Python language.

Python is often going to be described as simple and easy to learn, which is another reason why there is a big appeal for using it, whether you want to use Python with machine learning, or other data science systems. Some programmers are going to describe this language having a favorable complexity to performance trade-off, which makes it good to work with compared to some of the other coding languages. It is also more intuitive than a few other languages because of this syntax that is more accessible.

Other users like the point that Python has a lot of tools that can be great when working with a system of machine learning. Some cite that with all of the libraries and the frameworks that come with Python, including some of the extensions like NumPy, can make Python easier to implement in machine learning. So, the context of the language on its own is important when it comes to looking at why Python is the choice for machine learning.

Another resource that comes with Python, known as the scikit module is going to basically be the machine learning in Python that we are working with. This library is going to be the tool that professionals need to help make sure that Python is able to handle all of the tasks that are needed when it comes to machine learning.

Python, when compared to some of the other coding languages out there, including Perl, C, Ruby on Rails, or Java, is described in a more favorable manner when it comes to working with machine learning. Where some might decide to work with one of the other languages to help them out with hard coding, and they may even consider Python more of a toy language for just the most basic of users, many will find that Python is one of the best options, and it is a fully functional alternative to dealing with the cryptic syntax of some of the other coding languages out there.

As we can see here, there are a lot of benefits that come with using the Python language, and why it may be the best option to work with machine learning. The libraries that come with Python are one of the main reasons that Python works best with machine learning. There may be other programming languages to work with, but when you add in the functionality that comes with some Python libraries like NumPy, Scikit-Learn, TensorFlow, Pandas, and more, we can see that there are a lot of models and functions and algorithms that can make the work that we must do with machine learning so much easier.

Often Python is going to come in when it is time to work with data analysis. This analysis helps businesses to sort through all of the data that they have collected over time and provides them with predictions and insights that can lead to smart business decisions. Machine learning is able to create models that read through the data. And Python is able to read create the coding that comes with the models.

You can certainly choose to go with another coding language, and many of them do have the capabilities needed to handle machine learning. But when it comes to choosing a language that is easy, has a lot of power, comes with the libraries that you need to handle machine learning, and the community you need to take control if something goes wrong, then the Python coding language is the right choice for you.

There is so much that we are able to love when it comes to working with the Python coding language. There are many other languages that can help create programs and get some coding done. And there are plenty of programmers out there who have their favorite and will not use anything else. But when it comes to working with a language that is easy for beginners to catch on to, and that has the capabilities and the extensions to handle machine learning and any of the algorithms and models you need to sort through your data and find the best insights possible, then Python is going to be the natural choice.

With all of the benefits that we have talked about in this chapter, and how great Python is, it is likely that you are ready to dive in and create some of your own machine learning algorithms with the help of Python. So, let's get right to it!

# Chapter 4: Downloading the Best Python Libraries for Machine Learning

The next thing that we need to focus some of our attention here is the Python libraries. There are a lot of libraries and extensions out there that we can add to the Python library to extend out the capabilities of this coding language. And some of these are particularly good when you want to work with machine learning.

While there are a lot of great things that the Python language is able to do on its own, and the original library that comes with this coding language has a lot of power, there are still some spots that are lacking. For example, the traditional version of Python is going to be lacking in capabilities for scientific, engineering, and mathematical tasks. And since these are common parts that need to be included in a machine learning project and model, we need to add in a few extras to make this work for our needs.

The good news is there are a lot of extra libraries out there that work well with the Python coding language and can enhance this language so that it can handle some of the machine learning models that you want to work on. Some of the best Python libraries that can also handle machine learning will include:

# NumPy

The first library that we are going to take a look at is known as NumPy. If you want to do any kind of work with the Python language and with machine learning, then you will want to make sure that NumPy is on your list of choices to work with. Many of the algorithms that we are going to discuss later on will include NumPy so it is worth our time to learn more about how this one works and to take the time to download it along with Python.

To start with, NumPy is going to stand for Numerical Python, and this is a good indicator of what this library can do. When we take a look at the NumPy library, we will notice that is consists of multidimensional array objects along with a collection of routines that are meant to process all of these arrays. Using NumPy, you are able to work with logical and mathematical operations on arrays to get things done.

# SciPy

The second library that we can use with Python for machine learning is Known as SciPy. This is a free and open-source library that we can use with Python for some scientific computing, and for some technical computing as well. This can really help to extend out some of the technical tasks, and the scientific tasks that we are able to do with Python.

Some of the modules that we are able to use with SciPy will include signal and imagine processing, interpolation, optimization, integration, and linear algebra to name a few. These are all common tasks that we are able to work within the engineering and science fields, and when we add it to Python, it makes it easier to work with a nice library that can handle it all.

One thing to remember here is that the SciPy library is going to build upon the NumPy array object, and it is going to be included in the stack from NumPy which includes the SymPy, Pandas, and Matplotlib as well. These are all going to be used to help extend out the set of scientific computing libraries.

## Pandas

Another important library that we need to take a look at while we are on this topic is the Pandas library. This is another Python package that you can choose that is open-sourced and provides us with numerous tools to handle data analysis. The package is going to come with several structures of data that can be used for many different tasks of data manipulation. It will also come with a variety of methods that going to be used with data analysis, and this is very helpful when you are doing projects in Python that include machine learning and data science.

There are a number of advantages that come with using this Pandas library. Some of these benefits and advantages of working with the Pandas library in machine learning include:

1. This library can help to present data in a manner that is suitable to complete data analysis. This can be done through a few different data structures, including the DataFrame, and Series.
2. The package that comes with Pandas is going to include multiple methods to help us filter the data in a more convenient manner.
3. Pandas are going to have a variety of utilities to help us do operations of Input and Output in a manner that is seamless. It is also able to read data from a variety of formats including Excel, CSV, and TSV.

## Theano

We can also work with the Python machine learning library that is known as Theano. This is a machine learning library that will make it easier for us to define, optimize, and evaluate mathematical expressions that work with multi-dimensional arrays. This can be a big point of frustration for some programmers and developers when it comes to the other libraries that are available out there. This library can make the process of handling those arrays easier so you can use them to sort through your data and get the results that you would like.

Just like we will see with the Scikit-Library below, Theano can also integrate tightly with NumPy. The transparent use of the GPU is going to make Theano pretty fast and easy to set up, which is going to be a big benefit when it comes to starting out with the process. Although there are some programmers who have seen Theano and the tools that come with it as more of a research tool rather than something to use in production, it can still provide a lot of benefits to those who are just starting out with machine learning.

As you start to work with the Theano library, you will notice that one of the best features that come with it is going to be the great documentation and all of the tutorials to show beginners how to get things done. Thanks to the popularity of this library, it won't take long for you to find any resources or tutorials that you need to ensure that you can use Theano to get your models up and running the right way.

## Pylearn2

Most of the functionality that we are able to see with Pylearn2 is going to be built upon the library of Theano, so we know that it has a base that is pretty solid. Keep in mind that this library is going to wrap in other libraries when it makes the most sense to do this, so you may need to have a few of these libraries up and ready to go. This means that you won't get a code that is 100 percent custom-written all of the time.

The good news about seeing this happen though is that since you are getting pre-written code, it means that most of the bugs have already been worked out of the system. Wrappers like Pylearn2 do have an important place on this list and can ensure that you will be able to finish up what you need to in some of your machine learning projects.

## Pyevolve

When it comes to the world of data science and machine learning, neural networks are going to be a big arena that garners a lot of attention. And one of the more exciting, as well as different, areas of research into these powerful neural networks is the space of genetic algorithms.

To start with, a genetic algorithm is just going to be a search heuristic that will mimic the process that is known as natural selection. This means that it is going to test your new neural network on some data, and then will get some feedback on the performance of the network, going off the function of fitness. Then it will iteratively make some small and random changes to the network before going through another test again, and using the same data over again.

As this process goes through things over and over again, there is always going to be a winner and a loser, which brings in some competition to the code that you are trying to write out. Networks that have a fitness score that is higher will win out, and then it will turn into the parent that handles the rest of the new generations.

Pyevolve is going to provide programmers with a great framework that they can use to build and then execute this kind of algorithm to see the best results. Although the framework is also supporting some genetic programming that is being done, this is something that may be possible in the future but hasn't been explored as much as we need at this point.

## Pattern

When we work with the Pattern machine learning library, we will find that it is more of a full suite library compared to some of the others. This library is going to provide us with a few machine learning algorithms along with a few different tools that make it easier to collect and analyze the data that you have. The data mining portion that comes with this is going to be really helpful for us to collect data from some different sources like web services. These can include Wikipedia, Twitter, and Google.

This library is also going to have an HTML DOM parser and a web crawler. The nice thing that comes with these tools includes how easy it is to make it collect and train the data that you are using, both on the same program without having to change things up at all. This is a unique library that can handle so many parts of the data analysis process that you need to work on, and many companies are starting to see some more of the value, and some of the reasons why they will want to spend their time working with this.

## Caffe

Caffe is a library for machine learning that is going to work with vision applications. You might use it to create a deep neural network that will recognize objects in images or even recognize a visual style when it is needed. With this one, we are going to see seamless integration with GPU training which is going to be a great thing to use when you would like to train your data on images. Although this library is going to seem like it only works for things like research and academics, it can provide us with a lot of uses and benefits when we want to train models to use in production at the same time.

## Scikit-Learn

The next library that we are going to take a look at is the Scikit-Learn library. This is definitely going to be one of the most popular libraries out there for machine learning, no matter which coding language that you want to work with. It does work really well with Python as well, which is going to make it the perfect companion for a lot of the different codes that you want to write in this particular language.

The Scikit-Learn library is going to have a large number of features that make it work well for processes like data analysis and data mining. This alone is going to make it the perfect choice for developers and researchers who are working to go through all of the data that they have and form some meaningful insights out of that data.

With this library, we will find that it is built on top of a few other libraries that are popular for machine learning, including NumPy, SciPy, and Matplotlib, which means that it will come with a familiar feel if you have already worked with those libraries listed above. Although it is compared to some of the other libraries that we will talk about in this chapter, this one is seen as a lower-level library and tends to act as more of the foundation, rather than the main thing, for many of the different implementations of machine learning.

Even though this one may be more of a foundation for other machine learning libraries, there is still a lot of power that comes with it, and Scikit-Learn can help to power up a lot of the programs that you would like. Because of the power, it can be difficult to start with this library unless you are working with a good resource to get all of this done. You can use Scikit-Learn to help out with pretty much any machine learning process that you want so it is definitely a good choice to learn about.

# TensorFlow

Another library that you are able to use when it comes to Python machine learning is known as TensorFlow. This is one of the newest neural network libraries that are on the list. This is going to be one of the higher levels of neural network library that is meant to help you program your architectures for a network while avoiding some of the details that are lower level in the process. The focus with this one is going to be more on allowing us to expression some of our computation as a data flow graph, rather than relying on some of the other options. Because of this, the graph is going to make things easier to solve complex problems.

When it comes to TensorFlow, you will find that most of the coding and executing will be written out in C++, which is going to including the bindings from Python, so you won't have to worry about having a complicated coding language, or sacrifice your performance in the process. One of the features that will be a favorite for many programmers is that TensorFlow has a flexible architecture, which is going to allow you to deploy it to one, and sometimes more, GPU or CPU in a server, mobile device, or a desktop. And all of this can be done using the same API. Other programming libraries are not able to make this same claim at this time.

TensorFlow is also unique in that it was developed to work with the Google Brain project and it is a library is now used by engineers throughout the Google company, and other industries as well. This can show us how there is so much power with this library, and we should have no question about whether it is capable of creating some of the solutions that we need.

Like any of the other libraries in this chapter, you will need to take some time to learn the API, but the time spent with this library is definitely going to be worth it. Within the first few minutes of looking at the core features, you will be able to tell how TensorFlow is able to help a programmer spend more time implementing the designs that they want in the network, rather than having to fight with the API.

As we can see with this chapter, there are a lot of different Python libraries that are designed to work with machine learning. These libraries were often designed with the sole purpose of working with machine learning, though they will also work well with some of the other tasks that you will want to create as well. Take some time to look through these libraries and learn more about how they are able to help you with your coding, and why they are the best options to help you accomplish some of the tasks that are needed with your machine learning algorithm.

# Matplotlib

As you are working with machine learning, there are going to be times when you want to create a graph or another visualization of the data that you have analyzed. You could leave all of the data and the summaries in written form, but this is boring and often hard to read. Taking the data and turning it into some kind of visualization may be the key that you need to really make it easier to see the data, and to understand it better than before.

This is where the Matplotlib library is going to come into play. This is a library from Python that is meant to help with any plotting and graphs you would like to create. It comes in as a numerical mathematics extension of the NumPy library that we talked about before. In addition, the API that it provides is for an object-oriented format and will help embed the plots into the applications that you want to use. This is often done with a variety of toolkits of GUI including Tkinter, and wxPython.

Any time that we want to take a lot of data and then add in some graphs or other visualizations to go along with it, then we need to work with the Matplotlib extension. This one can help us get these visualizations done in no time, and will ensure that we are able to get some strong results, and some nice graphs and charts, in no time.

# Getting These Libraries Set Up

Now that we have had a chance to look at some of the best Python machine learning libraries that you can use it is time to move on to downloading these libraries and getting them ready to work on your system. The best part about this is that assuming you already have the Python code and all its folders on your computer already, it is easy to download the library that you would like to use for machine learning.

When you are ready, pick out the library, or libraries, that you would like to work within machine learning. We already took some time to explore a few of the best options that you can work with, so take a look at some of the benefits of each one, and the tasks that each one is able to handle, and then go with that option. After choosing the libraries that you want to work with, it is time to start the downloading process.

For this, just go to the main website for the library that you would like to install. These are going to offer free downloads of the libraries (the ones we talked about are open-sourced and free to download. If you choose to go with a different option there is a chance that they will charge a fee to use their library). You can go through the steps to make sure that the library is the right version, that you have a compatible operating system, and then click Next to start the library.

You will need to go through the download process each time that you want to download a new library. This will ensure that each library is on your system and ready to use. These may take a few minutes to download and get set up. But once that is done, you will be able to use the library and start some of your own machine learning projects in no time.

# Chapter 5: How to Use the Python Shell

So far in this guidebook, we have spent some time taking a look at what machine learning is all about and how we can work with the different types of machine learning to see some success based on the data that we want to process through, and what our end goals are for the project or the data. We also took a look at what Python is all about and why it is such a great coding language to work with, even with some of the more complex parts that come with machine learning algorithms.

Now it is time to take a bit of a detour to see more about the Python Shell, and how we can use this to our advantage. Learning how to write in the Shell, and how we can set it up, can be critical to how well our project does when we work with machine learning. With this in mind, let's dive right in and see more about what the Python Shell is all about.

## What is the Python Shell?

As we work through the Python language, we will see that it comes with a part that is known as the Shell. This often goes by the name of an interactive shell and the best way to think about it is the command-line interface of the program. If you would like to write out the codes for Python and machine learning, then you will be working with the Python shell.

There is a basic Python shell that comes up when you download the program and use it for your needs. However, there are several other options that you are able to work with as well. These will come from third-party developers and sometimes these are going to cost a bit more to use as well. But if you are using some of the special features that come with these, then it may be worth your time depending on what you would like to do.

The Shell is going to come in with a few different names based on what kind of operating system that you work with. With a Mac computer, you will work with the terminal. But if you are using a Windows computer, you will have the CMD. No matter what it is called on the computer you are using, you will see that this is a great place to start writing out some of the codings that you would like to do in Python.

When we are working on writing the Python code, there are two methods that we are able to work with. The first option here is to write out some of the code with Python in a .py file, and then run it inside the shell using the syntax of 'python filename.py'. What this is able to do for us is to execute the whole.py file at the same time and the result of that file is going to show up at the end of the code for us.

Then there is a second method that we are able to use. With this one, we will open up our shell and then write out the word "python". This is going to help us open up the interactive Python shell before we get started on the other things we want to get done. We need to make sure that we include the '>>>' with every line of code that we try to enter, but then you will be able to write the Python code that you want directly from here.

The main advantage of doing the code writing in this manner is that you are able to watch the result that you get with each line right after it is typed up. This may seem confusing, but many developers like to work with this method of writing code because it allows them to test their code, and see where mistakes and errors are going to show up right away.

Now, there are going to be a few things that we need to take a look at as we work through the shell. And these are going to include the difference between the script and the program. There are a lot of definitions out there about these two concepts and these two words, but we can take a little look at how these works and how they may affect what we are doing.

To start with, one of the main differences that come with a script and a program is that the script is going to be the part that is interpreted, and the program is the part that is executed. The source is first going to be compiled, and the result of that compilation is executed.

To make this a bit further, the scripts are going to be very distinct from the core code of the application, which is usually going to be written out in a different language. Then the end-user is able to create these, and sometimes modify these as they see fit. These scripts are often going to be interpreted by a bytecode or a source code, but then the applications that they are able to control will be compiled traditionally with the native machine code to make things easier.

On the other hand, we can work with a program as well. The program is going to be an executable form that the computer can look over and ten use in a direct manner in order to execute whatever instructions are there. the same program is going to have the source code form that is readable, from which an executable program can be derived out of that information.

There is so much that we are able to do with the Python Shell. Any time that you are looking to write up a program and create something new in terms of coding, the Python shell is going to be the place where you get all of this done. You can also work with several other third-party extensions to make this work the way that you want in the process.

## Some More Things to Do with Python

When we work with the Python coding language, we will find that there are a lot of options that we can work with and tasks that we can complete. With Python, you are able to make things like a math trainer that helps us to practices the time tables, and even create a simple encryption program or a secret code. And as you go through all of this and honed in your skills you will find that there are a ton of other things that you can do as well, including some of the tasks that come with machine learning.

Before we dive into all of that though, we can look at some of the fun things that come with coding in Python, and some of the more basic tasks that the Python Shell is able to help us out with. Some of these tasks will include:

1. Use sets of widgets to help us write out some useful applications that will use graphics instead of just text to help our program interact with the user.
2. Take some time to extend out other programs you want to use, like Blender, GIMP, and LibreOffice to name a few. You can do this by writing out some of your own custom scripts in the process.
3. You can write out games that have graphics with a few different libraries.
4. The Matplotlib library is a great one to work with because it helps us to draw some of the more complex graphs for any of the data you are collecting or the science and math courses that you are working within this process.

There is a lot that we are able to do when it comes to the Python code, and learning how to make this work for our needs can be very important to how much success we will see with the machine learning projects that we work on as well. Combining machine learning and Python can be easy, and when you learn all of the basic parts that come with the Python language, and how to use the Shell properly your projects are going to work the right way each time.

# Chapter 6: The Process of Handling Data Before Putting into Your Algorithm

Now that we have had a chance to talk about machine learning and a bit about Python, and before we dive into some of the best machine learning algorithms that you can write out with the help of Python, it is time for us to dive in to some of the processes that happen to help you handle any data you would like. Gathering the data is a great first step, but there are a number of other parts that need to come together so that the machine learning algorithm can actually ready, analyze, and offer insights on the data you are working with.

This process is going to take some time. And it isn't as much fun to work with as getting the insights and the predictions. But it is still an important part of handling this process. Without knowing how to deal with the data at hand, you will find that the algorithm will not make it through the training or the testing process, and if it does give you any results, there are no guarantees that those results are going to be accurate.

There are a number of steps that we need to take to make all of this happen and to ensure that we can get all of the insights and predictions that we need from our machine learning algorithms. We need to gather the data, clean off and organize the data, and handle any of the missing values or the duplicate entries that show up in the data. When that is done, it is time to train the model, test the model, look through the insights, and then create some visualizations to help us understand the data that we are looking at.

With this in mind, it is time to go through some of the steps that come with handling any data that we collect so that it can work with the algorithm and the machine learning model that we want to create.

## Gathering the Data

The first step that we need to work on when processing and handling data for machine learning is to actually get out there and gather the data that you need. The model will never work, and can't tell you any of the insights and predictions that you want to work with. So, collecting the data and finding it in the right locations, can be a critical first step to help us get started

Before we dive into that though, we need to figure out the big business question that we want to solve. This will depend on what your business is hoping to accomplish through this process. Are you looking to release a new product on the market? Are you looking to improve your marketing efforts? Do you want to stay ahead of the game and predict when a piece of equipment is going to break so you can fix it in time? Do you want to find a new niche or a way to beat out your competition in some other way? Decide how you want to use this model so you can go out and pick the data that will help you to reach this goal.

Now, it is possible that you have been collecting data for some time already, before coming up with a business question. This is fine. Still, take some time to figure out what that big business question is going to be. This helps you to select the right information to use for training and testing your data. You do not want to just throw all of the information you have at the model. This is going to overwhelm it, and the model will not know what it should do from this point. Selecting the data that will help answer your business question, can make a big difference here.

There are a lot of different sources that you are able to rely on when it comes to finding and gathering the data that you want to use with your Python machine learning model. You can choose to gather information on your customers, work with social media, send out surveys, and even use third-party studies and information to help you out.

This is going to be a lot of information that we need to gather in and look through. And it comes in a lot of different formats. This is just fine for this point because we will be able to clean and organize some of that information later on when it is time to create the model. Just work on collecting some good quality data that will help your model learn what you want, and then help you make good predictions and business decisions.

While we are here, consider where you would like to store all of the data that you collect. This is going to be a large amount of data, and it is often best to find some cloud computing or other software that you can use to hold onto that data. There are a lot of great options out there that you can work with for holding onto the data so do a bit of research and see which one is the best for you.

## Organizing and Cleaning the Data

As you will see as we go through this chapter, gathering the data is just the first step that has to happen with processing and handling data, and then putting that data through your chosen algorithm and model. We have to take that data and get it prepared to work with the model, and that is exactly where this step is going to start.

Our goal with this one is to organize and clean any of the data that we have been able to gather over time. We need the data to be in the same format to start with. If you have collected this data from a variety of sources it is possible that some of it are going to be in image form, some in video, some in text, and more. This is going to be a mess, and your algorithm is not going to know how to handle all of this turning all of this into the same format, and sorting through the data that you want to use can make a big difference in how well you can understand what is actually hidden in that data.

Remember the main point of doing data science, and using the various machine learning algorithms that we are going to talk about in this guidebook is to help us to sort through our data and learn some valuable insights. We know that this data is too vast for a human to handle on their own, and so we can use the Python machine learning algorithms to handle it all.

While using these algorithms can make a big difference in how easy it is to get through the data, we have to remember that they will not be able to sort through things quite the same as us. Humans can tell the difference between the images, the files, the text, and the videos, and any other format that comes up. But if you present all of these different data types to your algorithm, it is going to end with a mess. We need to make it as easy on the algorithm model that we create as possible, and organizing and cleaning the data before putting it through our model can be the best way to do this.

## Filling in Duplicates and Missing Parts

As you go through the data that you have gathered, and you work on cleaning and organizing the data, you may find that there are a few issues that show up in that set of data. This is not something to be overly concerned with. When you collect data from a wide variety of locations and sources, this is bound to happen at one point or another, whether the data is labeled or unlabeled.

Even though this is common, we still want to take the time to sort through it and fix any of the duplicates or the missing parts that are in your data. Leaving these inside the data, especially if there are quite a few of these present, can really mess with the data that you need to work with, and can make it harder to get accurate information out of your data set. Each of these mistakes or duplicates can tip the results one way or another, and learning how to get rid of them and minimize the impact that they can have on your training set can be important.

Let's first dive into the duplicates. There may be times when you gather information, and there ends up being some duplicates in your set of data. If there are too many duplicates present, this can present a problem in the algorithm you use. These duplicates are going to shift the results, and they may not be as accurate for the overall sampling of the data, and this is never a good thing

You can work with Python in order to limit the number of duplicates that are in your set of data. You don't have to go through and look at all of the data to find these duplicates. This would be too complicated and almost impossible. There are a number of codes that you can use that will look for duplicates and will limit them down to what you see as acceptable. Some programmers won't allow for any duplicates in the information, but others will be fine for one duplicate to show up there.

Now we can look at how we would handle some of the missing values that show up in the set of data that you are working with. There are times when you will collect your data and there will be missing values. There are a few ways that we are able to deal with this kind of problem. Some programmers like to work with the mean of the answers around it to fill in that spot. Others like to delete the listing overall so that it is no longer in the set of data.

What you do with this information is going to be based on what you want to find. Depending on your intended results, you may be able to find another creative way to deal with this missing information that will make your learning algorithm more successful overall. But make sure that you handle these missing values so that you can teach the model how to behave properly, and to ensure the most accurate results are going to show up.

One thing to note here is that you may look through some of the data and notice there are a number of outliers. Depending on what your questions are to the set of data, these outliers may be things that you ignore, and other times they can provide you with some valuable information that can really work to put your business ahead of the competition.

If you look at the data and only notice a few outliers, these are not that important and you could probably avoid them. Sometimes programmers will choose to eliminate some of these outliers to ensure they have no impact on the results they get out of the data set. It is up to you whether you want to keep these outliers in with the information or not.

Then there are times when these outliers can seem really important. If you are looking at the data, and you notice that there are a number of outliers, especially ones that collect together and seem to lean towards a certain trend, then this could be a new area for you to explore that you never considered in the past.

Maybe you are working with your data to separate out your target audience to see how you can reach them better. You find that most of the data fit into one cluster of individuals and that is the target audience that you have already been working with over time. But then you notice there are some outliers in there as well. Most of these may be random, and maybe they represent people who have bought something at your store as a present for someone in the target demographics.

Then you look a little closer and find that a small, but significant amount of the outliers fall into their own little cluster. Upon a closer look, you see that this shows another age group of individuals who may be interested in your product. Maybe you had sold to individuals who were between the ages of 18 to 22 but then this outlier cluster shows that there are people interested in your products that fit in the age group of 24 to 28.

What this means for your business is that you can then branch out and work with marketing and advertising to reach this other demographic. It could be a largely untapped group that would be interested in what you have to offer, if only they knew about you. Before the competition finds this out you can market to these demographics, make products that would appeal to them, and more, beating out others and really improving your business.

This can be done with any business question that you start out with. It can help you figure out places where you can reduce waste it can help you figure out the best new products to offer to customers. And it can help with a lot of the other questions that you have for your business. These outliers are not always going to mean something, and many times you can forget them and not look them over at all. But on occasion, it is worth your time to check them out.

## The Training Set

The next step that we need to take here is to train the model. You cannot just write out an algorithm to go with your model, and then assume it can handle any of the data that you want to use and will provide you with some results that are accurate and will work for you. You are basing a lot of important decisions for your business on this model, so taking the time to train it properly can be worth your time.

Picking out the right kind of data and inputting it to the model so that it can learn how to behave is going to be a critical step. Later we will take a look at how we can test the data after some of the training has been done. But first, we need to select the data that we want to use to help train our model so that it behaves in the manner that we would like.

The first thing that we need to look at with the training data is how accurate and high quality it is. You should not just throw any data that you have into the model, or it will give inaccurate results. Your goal is to find the data that is higher in quality and can provide the model with some accurate learning along the way. This can take a bit more time sometimes, but in the long run, it is worth your time to train the data set the right way, to ensure that you can actually get accurate results when you use it for real-life predictions, insights, and big business decisions.

We also need to determine whether we are going to use labeled or unlabeled data in this one. The type of data that we have already gathered is going to often lead us in the direction of picking out the right algorithm to create our model. Many times, it is easier to train the model with labeled data, but this takes longer to collect and is more expensive. There are plenty of models that we can work with that can handle unlabeled data. This may include a few more training rounds to get things right, but it opens the door to a plethora of data that you can use. You can be more selective with your choices and work from there in training your data.

Do not try to rush through this part of the model creation process. It is tempting to just send through a few rounds of data and assume the data is going to work just fine. But if your data is not accurate, and you aren't careful with the data that you are resenting to the algorithm, then it will not work the way that you were hoping. And the more that you can train the algorithm, with more examples that it can base its knowledge on, the more accurate that can come with the algorithm model.

## The Testing Set

After you have spent some time working through the model and training it through the steps above, it is time to work on a bit of testing. The goal of the training was to teach the model how to behave, and now we want to go through the right steps to make sure that the model is actually learning something, and that it can provide us with some accurate results in the process.

Think of it this way. When you were back in school, you would spend a number of days learning about a new topic in one of your classes. The teacher would spend some time showing you examples of those topics, discussing that topic, and maybe having you write on the topic and more. This would be like the teacher feeding you the training set to help you learn this information.

After some time though, the teacher would decide to test you on this information. They want to make sure that you are not just taking in the information and then ignoring it or forgetting it right after the fact. They want to see what you have been able to retain from the class, so they will test you on it This is what happens with the testing phase in machine learning.

It may seem like a long process, and many data scientists would prefer if they could just do the training part and skip over the testing part. But how are you supposed to know whether or not the model you have created actually works well or not if you haven't taken the time to test it first? It is never a good idea to just do the training, and then take the model and start using it for predictions and for making important business decisions.

There are a number of reasons for this one. The main one is that we have no idea how accurate the predictions are. If you fed the model some low quality or bad data in the training set, then it is possible that the testing results are going to come in lower than 50 percent. Since it is assumed that the machine should be able to guess and get half of the answers right, even without the training, this is a very bad thing. You do not want to risk your business and your future plans on a model that is not accurate.

There are a number of reasons why your model may test out at a lower accuracy, but usually, it is because of the type of data that you put in during the training. Remember for this we want high-quality data, or the algorithm model is not going to do what we expect, either during the training or the testing phase. We want to pick out the best data possible so that, at the very least, our model can be built up in the right way, and we can use it.

The goal is to also get the model to test with as much accuracy as possible. But since the algorithm is learning all of the time, it is possible that we could start out with a lower percentage of accuracy, and then see it build up in the process. The rule of thumb here is that we want the accuracy to be above 50 percent after the first test. It is an assumption here that if the model was just run on the data, without any training, it should be able to guess right at least 50 percent of the time. So, if you run a test and get a result like 60 percent, it may not be as high as you would like, but it is a good sign that the model is working.

If the accuracy is lower, then it is time to dive back into the training data and see what is wrong. This is usually due to some bad training data, not enough data, or low-quality data that you used for the training. Going through and being more careful about the data that you select, and adding in more training sets can help to make this better.

Even if the accuracy that you get from the training model is only a bit about half, that is a good sign. Doing a few more test runs, along with some more training in between can help you to get the accuracy much higher in the process. The more that the model can see information and go through the training process, the better it is going to get at completing some of the work that you would like to get done. And as long as the training data you are working with is good and high-quality, the accuracy of your model is just going to increase.

## Getting the Results

After the model that you create has had some time to go through its paces, and you have done the training and the testing phase, it is time to move on to getting the results. The point of this model is to use it to make predictions and smart business decisions that can help out in a lot of different ways. But if the model is not set up properly then it doesn't matter what you want to get out of the data, because it will end up being wrong.

If you have trained and tested the data in the right way, then this is not an issue for you. You can use the model as many times as you would like, and it is going to provide you with some amazing results and can help out with your decision-making needs. As the model is used more and more, the results that it gives will become more accurate. Remember that we are working with machine learning here so the program is designed to learn from its mistakes and get better.

Because of this, it is possible that some of the early results that you get may not be 100 percent accurate. Having that testing run before using the model on any major decisions can help here because it will start the training process and get the model a head start. But there may be a learning curve that comes into play with this at times as well.

In the first bit of time that you spend with the model, you may have to use some of your own knowledge as well, and you may find that you should go through a few more training and testing phases to increase the accuracy. Over time, it will get better and even in the beginning, if you used high-quality data and stick with it, you will find that you can still get accurate predictions and great insights to help your business to run.

As time goes on, the model is going to get better at its job, and you will see that the insights and the predictions that it provides are better than before. The more that you use the model, the more accurate it can become. Before you know it, you will be able to input any data that you want and get the right results to help you increase customer satisfaction, beat the competition, and even reduce the waste your business experiences.

# The Visualizations

The final step that we need to spend some time on here to ensure we are set with our data analysis, and with the machine learning algorithm that we use, is the data visualization. It is easy to get excited about the data and all of the other steps and race through this part assuming that we don't need to put it into a visual at all. But this part is just as important as some of the other choices out there, and spending some time taking all of that data and all of the insights that you have created, and turning it into a graphical form can make it easier to learn about the data at a glance.

Sure, we could just put the data and the insights into written form and hand it over to the key decision-makers for the company. And they would be able to learn some great information out of there. But adding in a few visuals about the information, to show the relationships between the points of data and how you came up with your predictions can make things easier.

Reading through all of that data can be time-consuming, and slows down the process. Sometimes it is hard to read through the information and figure out what is there. But if we put it into a chart or a graph, we can see the important insights as a glance. For those who may not be data scientists but who need to use this information in order to make some key decisions, the visualizations are going to be important.

So, once you have had a chance to go through some of the steps that we talked about above, it is time to dive right into creating some of your own visualizations as well. The kind of data that you are working with will help to determine the best visualization for your needs in most cases, so start with that to make it easier. Some of the various visualizations that you can choose from that work well with your data analysis will include:

1. **The line chart:** This kind of chart is there to show us some trends, accelerations, and the volatility of the process we are working on. This is a great way for us to take a look at the relationship in how data is able to change over a specified time period.

2. **Bar graphs:** There are three main choices that we can make when it comes to a bar graph. There is the stacked version, the column version, and the horizontal version. Although all of these are going to be found in the same family of charts, each one is going to serve its own purpose.

   a. **The horizontal bar graph:** These are going to be the best for things like comparative ranking, as a top-five list. They can be good for labeling data that is long.

   b. **Column graphs:** These are great when you would like to show something like chronological data, such as the amount of growth that happened over a specific period of time, and it can compare data that may happen across a lot of different categories.

   c. **Stacked charts:** These are going to be the kind that you use to handle the part to whole relationships. This would be when you would like to compare the data that you have, rather than actually seeing the total, and will usually be done in the form of a percentage.

3. **Pie charts:** This is a useful one to work with when you would like to demonstrate the proportional composition of a particular variable over a timeframe that is static.

4. **Scatter plot:** This is something that you would use any time that we want to find a correlation in a large set of data. The data sets have to show up in pairs with a dependent variable and an independent variable as well. The dependent one is going to turn into what we see on the y-axis and then the independent variable is the part that is found on the x-axis.

5. **Tables:** And finally, we can also work with tables on occasion. These are not necessarily a type of data visualization, but sometimes they can show your data in a way that just is not possible with some of the other options. This can help to keep the data organized and provides at a glance information on that data as well.

Working with data science and data analysis can be a great thing for most businesses. It ensures that we are not just collecting a large amount of data, but that we are also able to handle that data and get it organized to then learn the insights that we need. Machine learning can provide us with a lot of insights into the data that we collect, but we still have to take the time to learn how to handle our data and make sure that it is ready to go through the algorithms and models we are creating. The steps that are listed above can help us to get all of this done in no time.

# Chapter 7: Creating Your Own Neural Network

The first type of machine learning algorithm that we are going to explore is the neural network. This one is going to be a really great algorithm to work with because it fits under the category of unsupervised machine learning and they are designed to work in a manner that is similar to how the brain works. We will see this pop up in discussions of machine learning quite a bit because they will help us to look through a lot of data and find the patterns that are present inside of the data. This can be done at different levels, and in a manner that is much faster and more efficient than anything a data scientist could do manually or on their own without the system.

Any time that we want to create a neural network, each of the layers that we go through will spend a bit of time in that layer, exploring and seeing whether it can find a pattern in the image or object that it is looking at. Then, after finding a new pattern in that information, the neural network is able to start the process that is needed to go into the next layer. This process will continue, with one layer and then the next layer until all of the layers for the algorithm of neural networks are created and the program can provide us with a good prediction of what is found in that image.

When we reach this point in the process of the neural network, there are a few things that could happen, and this will depend on how you set up the program to behave. If the algorithm was able to go through those steps that we listed above, and it was successful with sorting through the various layers that are present, it is then going to make a prediction for us about what is hidden inside that image that you scanned.

If the prediction the neural network provides to us is right, the patterns in the system will remember this, and they will become stronger than ever for the next time. This happens due to the fact that the program is using artificial intelligence to make some strong associations between the patterns and the object. The more times that the system can do this process successfully and come back with an answer that is right, the more efficient the neural network will become each time that you try to use it.

Sometimes looking at an example of how this is meant to work is the best way to determine how the neural network can provide you with the results that you want. But with a closer examination of how all of this works, and how the neural network is able to help us see what is inside the image can be important to this process as well.

Let's look at an example of putting the neural network on an image of a car. The program that you are trying to create is to get the machine to look at a picture, using a neural network, and then make an accurate prediction of what is found in the image. The neural network will be able to do this because it looks through the pictures and goes through the various layers to learn something along the way. in the end, if the neural network is able to learn something along the way, it will see a car in the picture.

This program is going to be able to come up with an accurate prediction that there is a car inside the image that you present. This happens based on the various features that it sees in the image and is able to associate back to what comes with a car. This may include the color of the car, the license plate and the number that is on it, where the headlights and doors are located and more.

You may wonder if this is something that we could create with the traditional coding methods from before. It may be possible to create something that is like a neural network, but it is a difficult process to work with, and it would take a long time to complete. You will find that the systems of neural networks can make this so much easier, and you can create your own neural network in no time.

To get this neural network algorithm to do the job that you want, you need to first find a good image of a car and then present it to the machine. The neural network is then going to get to work and will take a good look over the picture. The algorithm would start with the first layer, which might be something like the edges of the car. Then, when it sees the new pattern that is there, it would continue on through some more layers.

This movement through the layers is what will help the neural network understand whether or not there are any unique characteristics present in the picture of that car. If the program is successful at going through all of the different layers and learning what is there, it is going to be able to see all of the smallest details that come with a car, including things like the wheel patterns and the windows, and it would make an accurate prediction.

There is the potential for many layers to come out of this one, but the more layers that our neural network can find, and the more details, the more accurately the system will be able to predict what kind of car is there in front of it. If your neural network can become accurate at identifying what kind of car model is in front of it, or even that the image actually includes a car, then it is able to learn from this lesson. It will remember some of the characteristics and patterns that showed up in the car model and can store them around for later. Then, if the algorithm sees this kind of image again, the prediction it makes will happen faster than before.

When you are working with this neural network algorithm, you will often have to choose one and then use it when you would like to be able to go through a large number of pictures and then find some of the most defining features that are inside of the neural network. For example, there is often a big use for this kind of thing when you want to create software that recognizes the faces of those who use the system.

All of the information that you need to create this kind of system would not be available at the time that you tried to create the method. But you are able to teach the system how to recognize the different faces that are needed with the help of a neural network. These neural networks can also be really effective when you would like to work with a program that can recognize animals, car models, and more, such as an image search on one of your favorite search engines.

As we can see here, there are going to be a ton of advantages that come with using neural networks with machine learning. One of the advantages that come with this is that when you use a neural network, you are going to have more control over the various statistics that come with the algorithm. This can be great news for programmers who are working on a very specific project that they want to get things done with.

Even if you don't start out with all of the statistics at hand, or you are not sure how to use all of the statistics, you will find that the neural networks can be used to make it easier to get any complex relationship in the data to show up for us to use it. This can be something that happens with both independent and dependent variables, even if the variables are considered nonlinear in nature.

This may not be the right method for a programmer to use all of the time, despite some of the benefits that are able to come with it. One of the biggest challenges that a programmer may see with the neural network, and why it is not something that you would necessarily want to use all of the time, is the high cost that comes with computing. For some businesses and for a few of the projects that you want to do with machine learning, the cost of computation is just going to be too high and the process takes too long, to make it worth our time to work with the neural networks.

Despite this fact though, the neural networks can be a great addition to your toolbelt of available algorithms. It is really a powerful and effective method to work within machine learning, and can take some of the complex parts and patterns that we want to work with, and turns them into reality. And depending on which library you decide to use to make these neural networks, you can add in a lot of different functionalities and features along with these as well.

The neural network is going to work in a manner that is similar to the human brain. The more that it completes a task, and the more times that the algorithm can get the answer right, the stronger the connections of the network, which can be like the neurons in the brain, will become. This means that the algorithm, when it is used properly and able to make the right predictions on images and more, the faster and more efficient the algorithm is going to become and the easier it is to use.

There are a variety of options that can come into play when it is time to work with neural networks in machine learning, and if you have a complete program that you would like to be able to recognize patterns and complex information on its own, then the neural network is the right option for your needs.

# Chapter 8: The K-Nearest Neighbor Algorithm

The next algorithm that we are going to spend some time on here is known as the KNN algorithm or the K-Nearest Neighbors. This is going to be a good example of a supervised machine learning algorithm so we can start to see how this works as well. When we bring out this algorithm it is helpful in searching through the data that is present for the k most similar examples of any kind of instance that you are working with.

Once you can make this happen with some kind of success, then the KNN algorithm will move on to look through that information and provide you with a nice summary of the information. Then the algorithm will use the results that you receive to make a few predictions that you can use to make smart and informed business decisions.

Any time that it is time to work with the KNN algorithm for your model, you may find that your learning is going to turn into something that is competitive. The reason that this happens, and why it works for the model that you are trying to create, is because there will be competition between the various parts of the data. Then, the winner, or the one that is the best based on the data that you have, will be the one that ends up in the prediction.

This particular algorithm is going to show up in a different way than some of the other algorithms that we will spend our time on in this guidebook. Be aware that some programmers find that this algorithm is more of a lazier approach to learning, mainly because, even though it provides you with some good information along the way, it is not going to create the models that you need. To make this one work, you have to actively go through and actively ask it for a new prediction before it does the work.

Depending on what information you would like to gather out of that data, and what situation you are working with, the fact that the algorithm waits for your commands to create a new model can be a good thing. This ensures that the data is only the kind that you want and that the data is relevant to the information that you want to learn about.

If the program was set up in a way that it just made a prediction on a regular interval, or made these predictions each time that you inserted some new data into your storage it may be helpful in some cases. But if you want to just have certain types of data get analyzed, or you want to make sure that it is only answering certain questions for you, then the way the KNN algorithm works is much better for this.

There are a couple of benefits that we are able to see when working on the KNN algorithm compared to some of the others. When you bring out this algorithm, it is easier to create a model that cuts through the noise that is found in your set of data. This noise is pretty common with any set of data that you work with, but the larger the data, the more noise that is present in it. Getting rid of the noise and the parts that are not necessary can be a great way for you to really see the insights and important things in the data, rather than getting distracted by all of the things that don't matter there

If you are working with a really large amount of data for your analysis, and you want to sort through it all at the same time, then the KNN algorithm is a great choice to rely on. Unlike a few other machine learning algorithms that are out there, this one is not going to be as limited on the sort of data that it can work with, and you will see success with using the KNN algorithm on large and small sets of data.

One of the larger issues that can come when we pull out the KNN algorithm is that some of the costs of computation are going to be higher. This is even truer any time that we try to compare it to other unsupervised or reinforcement machine learning algorithms that can do the same thing. The reason that we see these computational costs as being so much higher is due to the fact that the algorithm focuses on looking through all of the data points, rather than trying to cluster them together. If you have a lot of data points, this is going to drive your costs up.

## When Should I Work with KNN?

The first question that a lot of programmers have when they first get into this algorithm is when they should actually use it. You can use this algorithm to help out with problems of classification and regression to help make predictions, which can make it even more powerful than some of the other options that we will talk about.

With this in mind, most of the time programmers will pull this one out when they want to look at a problem of classification for the business. There are three main facts that we need to take into consideration when evaluating the KNN algorithm as a technique and these include:

1. The power of prediction that comes with it.
2. The time that it will take to do the work
3. How easy it is going to be for you to interpret any output that you receive form this algorithm.

When we compare the KNN algorithm to a few other machine learning algorithms, such as logistic regression, CART, and random forests, we will see that it is going to fair well with all of the considerations and parameters. Often this is a good algorithm to work with because it can be used to interpret any results that it provides to you, and the calculation of time is lower than some other choices.

## How to Get the KNN Algorithm to Work?

Now that we have had some time to talk about the KNN algorithm and why it is such a great choice from machine learning to use, it is time to move on to actually using this algorithm with some of the models we want to create. There are a few steps that we can follow to ensure the KNN algorithm works the way that we want, and these include:

1. Load the data into the algorithm for it to read through. The algorithm is not going to work at all if we aren't able to load up the data that is needed to help it learn.
2. Initialize the value that you are going to use and rely on for k.
3. When you are ready to get the predicted class, iteration from one to the total number of the data points that you use for training, you can use the following steps to help.

   a. Start by calculating the distance that is in between each of your test data, and each row of your training data. We are going to work with the Euclidean distance as our metric for distance since it's the most popular method. Some of the other metrics that you may choose to work with here include the cosine and Chebyshev.

b. Sort the calculated distances going in ascending order, based on their distance values.

c. Get the k rows from the sorted array.

d. Get the most frequent class for these rows.

e. Return back the class prediction.

## Why Should I Use the KNN Algorithm?

The next thing that we need to consider is why a programmer should consider working with the KNN algorithm in the first place. There are many different algorithms available out there, and they can do a lot of neat things with machine learning as well. With this in mind, why would we want to go with the KNN algorithm over some of the other options that are available? What makes this one unique to work with? Some of the benefits that come with the KNN algorithm, and that you won't be able to find with some of the other machine learning algorithms includes:

1. It can work well with problems, even if they are considered multi-class.

2. You are able to apply this algorithm to both problems that are regressive and those that are classification.

3. There aren't any assumptions that come up with the data. This ensures that you get the information that you want,

rather than having any assumptions in the place causing some issues.

4. It is an easy algorithm to work with. It is easy to understand, especially if you are brand new to the machine learning process.

However, there are more options for algorithms that you are able to work with because the KNN algorithm isn't going to be perfect in each and every situation that you go to. Some of the negatives that come with using the KNN algorithm includes:

1. It is going to be computationally and memory intensive expensive. If you don't have the right system and the right amount of space to work with, it is going to make it more difficult to see the results that you want from this algorithm.

2. If there are a lot of independent variables that you are going to work with, you will find that the KNN algorithm is going to struggle.

3. The KNN algorithm isn't going to work that well if you have any rare event, or skewed, target variables.

4. Sensitive to the scale of data.

# How Can I Find the K-Value?

The last thing that we need to focus on in this chapter is how to find out the value of K. Without this value, it is hard to get the algorithm to work the way that we want. One of the best ways that we can find out the value of K is to work with the process of cross-validation. It is important to bring out this cross-validation in order to estimate what is known as the error of the validation. This isn't too complicated to work with; we just need to hold onto a subset of the training from the model building process to use later.

Cross-validation, which we are going to set at a 10-fold validation for this part, is going to involve the programmer going through the data they have, and then randomly dividing it up so that the training set has a total of 10 groups. You can have more or less based on what works for you, but since we are doing 10-fold validation, we need to have ten groups here.

As we are creating these groups or folds, we need to keep them as close to equal in size as we can. From that, 90 percent of the data in the groups will be used to train the model that you are using with the algorithm. The other ten percent is not wasted though. This is going to be used in the testing phase to help us validate the model and make sure that the model and the algorithm are working the way that we want.

With this in place, the rate of miscalculation is going to be computed using that ten percent, the same ten percent that we saved back from the original data in order to validate the model. This procedure has to go through and repeat itself ten different times, with 90 percent of the data being used to build the model, and ten percent is the testing phase, with each of the folds that you have. With the tenfold that we are talking about, this means we have to build up the model and test it ten times.

Each of the observations that you get from the groups that are run will be treated like they are the validation set, and you need to go through this process ten times to use up all of the data. When this is done, you will get ten estimates on the validation error. The algorithm can help us to average these out to get the best results.

# Chapter 9: The K-Means Clustering Algorithm

The next algorithm on the list that we are going to focus on for a bit is known as the K-Means clustering algorithm. This is going to come with a basic idea for machine learning but it can still help us when it is time to see the various trends and other things that should show up in the data you work with. The basics that we are going to see with the K-Means clustering is that it will take all of that large amount of data that you are working with and that is not labeled, and then puts them together into a group based on other similar data points.

Clustering is going to be another example that we can learn for unsupervised machine learning. This example is going to be applied when the data that you have doesn't contain any labels on it to work with at all. The goal with the K-Means clustering algorithm is to ensure that you are able to identify the clusters or the groups that are found in the data for your own needs.

The reason that we want to work with these clusters on our data is that any of the points of data, or the objects, that fall into the same cluster are going to be ones that share a lot of similarities to each other. On the other side of things, the items in the same cluster are not going to share that many similarities to the points in other clusters. The similarities that we see in one cluster is going to be the metric that a programmer can use to learn the strength of the relationship between the items in that cluster.

As a programmer, you may need to use clustering often when you work with data mining, especially the kind of data mining that is exploratory. It could also have some more uses including in the fields of pattern recognition, machine learning, information retrieval, image analysis, data compression, bio-informatics, and computer graphics to name a few.

The K-Means clustering algorithm is going to help us to form some of the clusters of data, and these clusters are formed based on how similar the values of data are. You will then need to go through and specify what you would like the value of K to be in these algorithms. Basically, the value of K is going to be the number of clusters that you would like to put the data into. If you want to separate your target audience by gender, then you would have two clusters for this. If you would like to separate the users out by their age, there may be a few more of these clusters.

The K-Means clustering algorithm is going to start out by selecting what it would like to have as the centroid value of the clusters that you work with, based on how many clusters you choose and how much data you are working with. And then there are three steps that the algorithm goes through, taking them in an iterative manner, including:

1. You will want to start with the Euclidian distance between each data instance and the centroids for all of the clusters.
2. Assign the instances of data to the cluster of centroids with the nearest distance possible.
3. Calculate the new centroid values, depending on the mean values of the coordinates of the data instances from the corresponding cluster.

## How to Work with K-Means Clustering?

The next thing that we need to take some time to look at here is how to work with this kind of algorithm. For this one to work, the input that we want to focus on for the k-means is just going to be a part of the matrix X. In many cases, you will be able to add in some organization to the choice that you make to ensure that each of the rows that are created will be a different sample, while each of the columns that show up in this matrix are going to include a new kind of factor or feature based on the code that you are creating. To ensure that this process does happen, there are two main steps that we need to follow to get the k-means algorithm to perform.

The first step that we need to work on allows the programmer to choose the centers that work the best for all potential clusters. If you are not sure about where to put these centers or where they are going to work the best, it is fine to start out with a good estimate of where they should be and focus on that as the venter. If you are working with this model and things are not lining up the way that you would like, it is easy to go back through the process and adjust the center later on.

The second part of this process is going to be working with the main loop. After you have had some time to choose your centers, it is time to make a decision about which cluster each of the points in your set of data belongs to. You can look through all of the samples that are presented to you, and then choose the center of the cluster that will fit in with this one the best.

From this part, you can then work on re-calculating the different centers of the clusters you want to work with. You will want to make the readjustments based on the center points that you assigned to each part. This is going to be a simple process to work with because all that it needs to have happened is for the programmer to take all of the samples, and then see where the means of these are. And once you have that answer, you have your own k-mean to work with on the coding.

This is a process that you will continue to do until the algorithm gets to the point of convergence. This happens when there are no more changes that can happen to the centers or assignments of the clusters. For the most part, programmers are able to get this done within five-step, if not less. You may notice that this is a different process than what we have with a gradient descent that is used in deep learning. The gradient descent is a process that can go through a lot of iterations to get the convergence, but the k-means usually only takes a few to reach the results.

# Doing Some of the Coding

Now that we know a bit more about what the K-Means clustering algorithm is about, and some of the ways that a programmer is able to use it to help them create the right solution for their programs, it is now time to go a bit further and implement these ideas and put together some Python code with this machine-learning algorithm to see how it really works. And we are able to do this through the implementation of the soft k-means through Python code.

To ensure that the coding is going to work, you want to make sure that you are going with what is known as the standard imports, and we need to make sure that they can work well with the utility functions. This is basically going to be the same thing as what we get with the Euclidean, along with the cost function. The formula that you can use to make this happen will be below:

*import numpy as np*
*import matplotlib.pyplot as plt*


*def d(u, v):*
    *diff = u - v*
    *return diff.dot(diff)*

```
def cost(X, R, M):
    cost = 0
    for k in xrange(len(M)):
        for n in xrange(len(X)):
            cost += R[n,k]*d(M[k], X[n])
    return cost
```

After we get to this part of the code, we have to take the time to make sure the function is defined so that it is able to run this algorithm before plotting the result. This is going to be a good thing because it is going to end up providing us with a scatterplot. This is where we will see the color will represent how much of that membership is inside of a particular cluster. The code that we would use to make this happen includes:

```
def plot_k_means(X, K, max_iter=20, beta=1.0):
    N, D = X.shape
    M = np.zeros((K, D))
    R = np.ones((N, K)) / K

    # initialize M to random
    for k in xrange(K):
        M[k] = X[np.random.choice(N)]

    grid_width = 5
    grid_height = max_iter / grid_width
    random_colors = np.random.random((K, 3))
    plt.figure()
```

```
costs = np.zeros(max_iter)
for i in xrange(max_iter):
    # moved the plot inside the for loop
    colors = R.dot(random_colors)
    plt.subplot(grid_width, grid_height, i+1)
    plt.scatter(X[:,0], X[:,1], c=colors)

    # step 1: determine assignments / resposibilities
    # is this inefficient?
    for k in xrange(K):
        for n in xrange(N):
            R[n,k]  =  np.exp(-beta*d(M[k],  X[n]))  /  np.sum(
np.exp(-beta*d(M[j], X[n])) for j in xrange(K) )

    # step 2: recalculate means
    for k in xrange(K):
        M[k] = R[:,k].dot(X) / R[:,k].sum()

    costs[i] = cost(X, R, M)
    if i > 0:
        if np.abs(costs[i] - costs[i-1]) < 10e-5:
            break

plt.show()
```

Notice as we are going through this code that both the R and the M will be in the matrix. The R is going to become the matrix here because it is going to hold onto the two indices, the k, and the n.

Then we have the M as well and this is another matrix that we can work with. This is due to the fact that it is going to contain the K individual D-dimensional vectors for us.

The beta variable that sows up with this one is going to control how spread out or how fuzzy the membership of the cluster can be, and we are going to call this our hyperparameter. From here, we are then able to create a main function that is responsible for handling our random clusters, and then we will call up the functions that we have been able to define above. The code that is needed to make this happen includes:

```
def main():
    # assume 3 means
    D = 2 # so we can visualize it more easily
    s = 4 # separation so we can control how far apart the means
are
    mu1 = np.array([0, 0])
    mu2 = np.array([s, s])
    mu3 = np.array([0, s])

    N = 900 # number of samples
    X = np.zeros((N, D))
    X[:300, :] = np.random.randn(300, D) + mu1
    X[300:600, :] = np.random.randn(300, D) + mu2
    X[600:, :] = np.random.randn(300, D) + mu3
```

```
# what does it look like without clustering?
plt.scatter(X[:,0], X[:,1])
plt.show()

K = 3 # luckily, we already know this
plot_k_means(X, K)

# K = 5 # what happens if we choose a "bad" K?
# plot_k_means(X, K, max_iter=30)

# K = 5 # what happens if we change beta?
# plot_k_means(X, K, max_iter=30, beta=0.3)


if __name__ == '__main__':
    main()
```

With all of this in place, we can now work with a model for K-Means clustering. This algorithm can help us to sort through all of the information that we have and then provides us with some of the clusters, and the necessary insights, that we hoped to gain from that information. Thanks to all of the clusters that are formed, we can get a good look at where our information is, how it relates to one another, and even some information on a few of the outliers as well.

# Chapter 10: How to Work with a Support Vector Machine

We have now taken a bit of time to look at a variety of methods that are useful when it comes to working with machine learning and the Python coding language. But now we are going to look at one of our last examples and see just how great Python can be with some of these projects. In this chapter, we are going to focus on the machine learning algorithm that is known as SVM or support vector machine.

The SVM is going to be something that a programmer is able to use to help them face a lot of the challenges that show up with classification and regression. With this algorithm, a lot of the work that has to be done on any problems of classification can end up turning the project into a tricky mess if you are not careful. But the algorithm for SVM is going to be the best option to help you ensure that you can handle all of the challenges that may come up with these problems.

When it is time to bring out some of the SVM algorithms in machine learning, there are a few steps that we need to take. To start with, the programmer has to take each of the items in the set of data and then plot them on a graph, turning them into an n-dimensional space. N is going to be important because it is going to be the number of features that you would like to use to finish up this project and get some insights out of the data.

From here, we are able to take the value that we decided on for all of the features and make it our goal to translate this over to the value that shows up on our coordinates. The job that we can do at this point will be to determine the hyperplane because this is the part that we will see show up on the graph, and it is basically the differences that show up between the classes that we are creating here.

At this point in the process, you may notice that the algorithm of SVM is going to sometimes offer us more than one support vector to choose from. It is not uncommon to see more than one option for you to work with, and for a beginner who is not used to this process, this can be confusing and a bit of a challenge. You want to make sure that you are picking out the right support vector, but with more than one option, it is going to be hard to know which one to choose.

The good news here is that many of them are going to not matter that much and you can easily see that they are just coordinates that show up based on the individual observations that you are able to see. You can then use the SVM to be the frontier that helps you separate out the vectors into classes. There are two main ones of these that we need to focus our attention on and these include the hyperplane and the line.

As we read through the above information, a lot of what we are talking about may seem a bit confusing and it may not make as much sense as it should. In addition, a beginner in programming with Python and machine learning may not know why we would want to waste our time on SVM and all the complications and challenges that come with this coding language. We have to remember that there are a few steps that we can work with on the SVM algorithm in order to get it to work in the proper manner and to ensure that this algorithm will properly sort out any of the data that we have.

The first step that we need to focus on here is going to be taking a look at the hyperplane. As we go through with this process, this is where we will notice that more than one hyperplane is going to show up at a time, and we need to pick from the one that works the best for our needs. We can add to this that there is the extra challenge that we have to make sure that out of these options, you are not picking out the wrong hyperplane and basing all of your information and data on that one part.

This can seem a bit scary for someone who is just getting started with this kind of algorithm and using it to build up a machine learning model. But the good news here, and another thing that we need to discover, is that even if you do look at this algorithm and the charts that come with it, and you notice that there are a few options present, there are a few easy steps that you can take that will increase the likelihood that you will pick out the right hyperplane out of the bunch. The steps that you can take include:

- We are going to start out with three hyperplanes that we will call 1, 2, and 3. Then we are going to spend time figuring out which hyperplane is right so that we can classify the star and the circle.
- The good news is there is a pretty simple rule that you can follow so that it becomes easier to identify which hyperplane is the right one. The hyperplane that you want to go with will be the one that segregates your classes the best.
- That one was easy to work with, but in the next one, our hyperplanes of 1, 2, and 3 are all going through the classes and they segregate them in a manner that is similar. For example, all of the lines or these hyperplanes are going to run parallel with each other. From here you may find that it is hard to pick which hyperplane is the right one.
- For the issue that is above, we will need to use what is known as the margin. This is basically the distance that occurs between the hyperplane and the nearest data point from either of the two classes. Then you will be able to get some numbers that can help you out. These numbers may be closer together, but they will point out which hyperplane is going to be the best.

The example that we went through with the steps above is only one example of a time when you would find the SVM algorithm and see it as a useful tool that helps out with machine learning. When you look through the various points of data that you have available, you will see that with the SVM method, there is a good margin that the points will separate from each other here, and the SVM method is going to make sure that we can handle this kind of work in no time at all.

In addition to some of the effects that we are able to see with this algorithm and machine learning model, will end up with an increase any time that you have a project with dimensional spaces that are going to be seen as higher than what is considered normal. There are times when this algorithm will not be the best option for you to work with, but even during these times, you will still be able to find other benefits and more of using this algorithm.

While there are benefits that you will get with this method depending on the project that you are working on, there are still going to be some times when the SVM method is not the best for you. When you work with a data set that is large, the SVM may not provide you with options that are the most accurate. The training time with these larger sets of data can be high, and this will disappoint you if you need to get through the information quickly. And if there are some target classes that are overlapping, the SVM is going to behave in a way that is different than what you want.

# Chapter 11: Decision Trees and Random Forests

The next topic that we are going to take a look at working with will be the decision trees and the random forests. These are going to be times when you will need to bring these out because they work to compare a lot of different possibilities and choices, and shows you the likely outcome that you are able to get with each decision that you have to make. The decision tree is going to include just one look at one choice that you want to make, and the random forests will include a bunch of these decision trees together, which can make it easier for us to work with a bunch of decisions that we want to make.

In this chapter, we are going to spend some time looking at these random forests, and the different parts that have to come together in forming good decision trees before turning it into a random forest. These may sound confusing, but we will find that they are one of the best ways to look through your information and see what the results of a variety of decisions will be.

## Decision Trees

The first algorithm that we are going to take a look at here is known as the decision tree algorithm. The decision tree is going to be an efficient tool to help out with data, especially if you want to work with more than one choice that you have to make, when the choices end up being very different from one another, and then use any of the information that you can gather to make the right decisions. The decision tree will provide you with the choices and the potential outcome that is with all of them, and ore.

When the decision tree is able to work well, it will lay out all of the decisions that you are trying to make and present you with the best outcomes that will come from each of those choices. This is going to help the programmer to see which decisions are the best to make and can ensure that it is easier to come up with the predictions that will help you to see success with your decision-making process.

There are a few ways that you are able to work with the decision trees. Many of those in machine learning like to use it either for variables that are categorical, or the ones that are random. However, in many cases, machine learning is going to ask you to use these decision trees to help with any classification problem. To ensure that you are coming up with a good decision tree, you will need to take up all of the data sets that you are working on and then splitting them up into two or more sets, with similar data in each set. These can then be sorted out with the help of the independent variables because this is going to distinguish them out from the different sets.

So, that brings up the question that this seems hard to make work. In order to make sure that this is all going to work well, you will need to take a look at an example, start out this exercise with the idea that there are 60 people in the class. All of these students will have three variables that are independent. These variables are going to include their class, gender, and their heights. When you take a look at the students who are in the class, you will know before you start that there are 30 of them that like to spend their time playing soccer.

Going from this information about which students like to play soccer, you decide that you want to create your own model so that you can figure out which half of the students in that class like to spend some time playing soccer, and which half of the students in the class don't spend their time playing soccer.

To figure out how to create the model that you want, your decision tree will need to take a look at all of the students that you have present, and then divide them up into the right groups. The variables that you would use here would include the class, height, and gender from before. The hope is that when you are all done, you are able to present a homogenous set of students who enjoy doing the same things.

Now, it is important to note that there are a few other choices of algorithms that a programmer is able to work with when they want to get the decision tree to work. And these algorithms are definitely not going to cause any harm with what you are doing. In fact, they are going to help make it easier to take the data that we are working with and split it up for working with.

This process is going to ensure that we have the right subsets to work with for the training and the testing process, and they can help to produce outcomes that are good, and outcomes that are nice homogenous, and help you to make the best decisions for your needs. Remember that it is possible for us to have more if the situation calls for it, but in this example, we are working with just two groups at this time. the first one will include those students who like to play soccer, and then the second one is going to consist of the students of those who don't.

You may find that while you are working with this algorithm, there can be some situations where you have to work with data that is more complex, and the decision tree can help you to sort things out based on the differences and similarities. The decision tree algorithm is going to provide us with a lot of the data that is needed here. And then the business can take all of that data they are working with, and make decisions that are smarter and more informed for the future of their business.

Sure, in the past business owner are able to use your intuition and this could be enough to make some of the decisions that your business needs. But there is just so much that has to come with the modern world and grow your business, so it just isn't possible to have this happen any longer. We have to take some of these algorithms, including the decision tree and the random forest and put them together to help make decisions, rather than relying on the intuition that could lead us wrong.

There are many times when a programmer will be able to work with machine learning and these decision trees to make it easier for us to make some smart business decisions. Learning how to make all of this come together can be one of the best decisions and predictions that are needed can make a difference in the benefits that you will see with the decision tree algorithm.

## Random Forests

Now that we know a bit more about these decision trees, it is time for us to move on to working with what is known as the random forest. There are times when the decision tree feels like it would fit with the goals that you have, but then there is something that is not quite right with this algorithm. When this happens, it may be time to bring out the random forest and see if you can make this one meet your needs.

These random forests are going to be popular to work with when it is time to make a good decision, so if you plan to use machine learning on your data on a regular basis, or you would like to get more into the field of working with data science and doing a data analysis, then taking some time to learn about the random forest and how it relates to the decision tree is going to be really helpful for your goals.

Since these random forests are a popular and pretty well-known algorithm to work with. It is not too hard to see that these algorithms have a lot of potentials to help a business take a bunch of potential decisions and then use the random forest to see what information and predictions will happen here. If you are looking to work with some tasks that explore through the data, like dealing with values that are missing or dealing with a few of the outliers that are in the information set you are working with, then the random forest is a great machine-learning algorithm to focus on.

There will actually be a few choices that come with machine learning where the random forest is going to be one of the best options to help you out. the reason for all of these reasons is because the random forest can be the perfect algorithm to provide you with any results that you need. And these algorithms are better at doing the job for much of the data analysis compared to some other algorithms. Some of the methods and steps that you can look for when it is time to figure out how to use the random forest algorithm will include:

- When you are working on your own training sets, you will find that all of the objects that are inside a set will be generated randomly, and it can be replaced if your random tree things that this is necessary and better for your needs.

- If there are M input variable amounts, then m<M is going to be specified from the beginning, and it will be held as a constant. The reason that this is so important because it means that each tree that you have is randomly picked from their own variable using M.

- The goal of each of your random trees will be to find the split that is the best for the variable m.

- As the tree grows, all of these trees are going to keep getting as big as they possibly can. Remember that these random trees are not going to prune themselves.

- The forest that is created from a random tree can be great because it is much better at predicting certain outcomes. It is able to do this for you because it will take all prediction from each of the trees that you create and then will be able to select the average for regression or the consensus that you get during classification.

The random forest algorithm is a great tool for a programmer to use when they would like to add in a bit of the power and techniques with data science with machine learning, and there are going to be a bunch of advantages to choosing the random forest algorithm compared to some of the other algorithms out there. The first benefit that comes with this algorithm is that it is able to deal with all of the problems that come up in machine learning, whether they are classification or regressions. When you take a look at some of the other algorithms that we talked about in this guidebook, they tend to work with either regression problems or classification algorithms.

The second benefit that comes with this kind of algorithm is that they are perfect when you have a set of data that is really large that you would like to deal with. This algorithm is able to handle hundreds of thousands of data points and various variables without trouble and without needing some extra power behind it either. It can take all of that information and give you some of the answers that are needed in the process.

This means that you can send in an almost unlimited number of data into this algorithm and it will do just fine. Your data set can be any size that you would like, but knowing that the algorithm can work no matter how big or small your data set is can make things easier. It is nice to know that before starting, there is enough power with the random forest to handle all of that data without freezing or delays.

Before you decide to jump on in and using random forests though, we have to remember that while these algorithms are able to handle all of the machine learning problems, including regression problems, they will not be able to make any kinds of predictions that go past whatever training data that you add into it, or the ranges that the programmer adds to the model in the first place.

This means that the random forest can help you to make some of the predictions that you need, and they will help you to figure out the best business decisions ever. But this is only up to the point where your data is able to go. If you want a prediction that goes well into the future, then this is not the algorithm for you to use.

As we can see there are a lot of times when we would want to work with machine learning and the various parts that come with the decision tree and random forest algorithms. These are both great options for making great decisions because it allows us to gather up our data and look to see how that information will compare. This makes it so much easier to compare the various decisions that we have to make and see which one is likely to give us the best outcome out of them all.

# Conclusion

Thank you for making it through to the end of *Learning Coding with Python*, let's hope it was informative and able to provide you with all of the tools you need to achieve your goals whatever they may be.

The next step is to start seeing how machine learning is going to be the tool that you need to see success with your business. There is so much that machine learning is able to help a business achieve. Sure, most businesses know that collecting data from a variety of sources is a good thing, but often they are stuck on which steps they should take afterward in order to see success. With the help of machine learning and the Python language, you will be able to take all of that data you have gathered, and learn some powerful insights that can help your business so much.

As we work through machine learning, there are a lot of complex tasks that can take a lot of time and can be hard to learn how to use. But with the help of the Python language, and some of the different algorithms that we discussed in this guidebook, we can take some of the challenges out and actually see machine learning work for our needs. That is exactly what we aim to do with the help of this guidebook.

When you are ready to see what machine, learning is able to do for your business, and you are ready to learn how Python can make all of this happen in no time, make sure to check out this guidebook to see exactly how to get started.

Finally, if you found this book useful in any way, a review on Amazon is always appreciated!

# Description

Are you interested in learning more about machine learning and what it is able to do for your business? Have you heard about some of the machine learning benefits, and you want to know how your own company will be able to benefit from it as well? Are you interested in learning the best insights, predictions, and more that can help you to make some of your own best decisions to grow your business and see some success?

Machine learning is one of the biggest buzzwords that we are looking at in many businesses and many different industries. It is the best tool for helping us to really learn more about the data that has been collected, and in ensuring that we are able to really make some smart business decisions. No matter where we see our business in the future, machine learning and some of the models that we are able to create with this technique will be able to help you out.

This guidebook is going to take some time to talk about machine learning, and how the Python coding language can help us to get some of these tasks done. Machine learning and the models that we are able to create with machine learning can really make a difference in how a business can run itself, and with the help of the Python language, we can put it all together and make some of the best business decisions for success.

Some of the different topics that we will discuss in this guidebook when it comes to Python and machine learning includes:

- What machine learning is all about
- The basic types of machine learning and some of the algorithms that can work with these learning types.
- The basics of the Python language and why it is considered one of the best for machine learning.
- Some of the simple steps that you can follow to ensure that your data is organized and ready for your machine learning algorithm.
- Some of the best machine learning algorithms to help us sort through our data and learn more about it, including Clustering, Neural Networks, and Decision trees!

There is so much that the Python language can do when it is time to pull out a complex task like machine learning, and put it to work. With the help of both of these features, we are able to handle the large amount of data that we have and can use it to come up with some of the best insights and predictions to guide our business. When you are ready to learn more about Python machine learning, take some time to read through this guidebook today!

Printed in Poland
by Amazon Fulfillment
Poland Sp. z o.o., Wrocław

52295571R00078